iCloud Guide

A Step by Step iCloud Manual

with Expert Tips & Tricks

Binary Press

1st Edition

© Copyright 2023

All rights reserved

The contents of this book may not be reproduced, duplicated, or transmitted without the direct written permission of the author. Under no circumstances will any legal responsibility or blame be held against the publisher or any reparation, damages, or monetary loss due to the information herein, either directly or indirectly.

Legal Notice:

You cannot amend, distribute, sell, use, quote, or paraphrase any part of the content within this book without the consent for the author.

Disclaimer Notice

Please note the information contained within this document is for educational and entertainment purposes only. No warranties of any kind are expressed or implied. Readers acknowledge that the author is not engaging in the rendering of legal, financial, medical, or professional advice. Please consult a licensed professional before attempting any techniques outlined in this book. By reading this document, the reader agrees that under no circumstances is the author responsible for any losses, direct or indirect, which are incurred as a result of the use of the information contained within this document, including, but not limited to, errors, omissions, or inaccuracies.

Table of Content

CHAPTER I: INTRODUCTION — 12

A Brief History and Evolution of iCloud — 12
- Predecessors and Early Concepts — 12
- The Birth of iCloud — 13
- Core Principles and Functionality — 13
- Evolution and Iterations — 14

Importance of Cloud Services in Today's Digital World — 14

CHAPTER II: WHAT IS ICLOUD — 17

Core Functionalities and Services Offered by iCloud — 17
System Requirements for iCloud — 19
- macOS — 19
- iPhone, iPad, iPod Touch — 19
- iCloud on Windows PC — 20
- Web Access — 20
- iCloud.com — 20

Storage Plan Requirements — 20
- iCloud Storage Plans — 20

CHAPTER III: HOW DOES ICLOUD WORK? — 21

Synchronization Across Apple Devices — 22

DATA STORAGE IN ICLOUD ----- 24

SECURITY MEASURES IN ICLOUD ----- 25

ICLOUD FEATURES AND SERVICES ----- 26

COLLABORATION AND SHARING: ----- 27

CHAPTER IV: HOW TO SETUP ----- 28

APPLE IDS ----- 28

MULTIPLE APPLE ID ----- 28

IMPLICATIONS OF SHARING AN APPLE ID ----- 29

CHOOSING THE RIGHT APPLE ID FOR ICLOUD SERVICES? ----- 30

SET UP ICLOUD ----- 31

SET UP ICLOUD ON A MAC ----- 32

SET UP ICLOUD FOR WINDOWS ----- 34

SET UP ICLOUD IN IOS OR IPADOS ----- 37

WORK WITH MULTIPLE ICLOUD ACCOUNTS ----- 39

USE MULTIPLE ICLOUD ACCOUNTS ON A MAC ----- 40

USE MULTIPLE ICLOUD ACCOUNTS ON AN IOS OR IPADOS DEVICE ----- 41

SWITCH PRIMARY AND SECONDARY ACCOUNTS ----- 42

DISABLE ICLOUD ----- 43

DISABLE INDIVIDUAL FEATURES ----- 43

DISABLE SERVICES FOR A SECONDARY ACCOUNT ----- 43

REMOVE A DEVICE FROM FIND MY DEVICE ----- 44

REMOVE AN ITEM FROM FIND MY ITEM ----- 46

CHAPTER V: HOW TO USE ICLOUD+ — 48

Setting Up iCloud+ — 48

Features Included in iCloud+ Tiers: — 50

Tier Variations: — 51

iCloud vs. iCloud+: — 51

Maximizing Storage Capacity — 51

iOS or iPadOS Device: — 52

Automatic Renewal: — 53

Family Sharing: — 53

Exploring Private Web Browsing — 53

The Two-Server System: — 53

Encryption and Data Handling: — 54

Maintaining Anonymity: — 54

Additional Protection: — 54

Activating and Customizing iCloud Private Relay — 55

On iOS/iPadOS: — 55

On macOS: — 55

Disabling iCloud Private Relay: — 56

Hide Your Email Address — 56

Mail App Integration: — 58

Setting Up a Custom Domain: — 58

CHAPTER VI: USE ICLOUD FAMILY SHARING — 61

Enable Family Sharing 62

Setting Up Apps and Services 64

A Guide to Apple School Manager Customizations 66

Manage iCloud Features and App Access: 67

In Apple School Manager: 68

A Guide to Apple Business Manager Customizations 69

Managing iCloud Features and App Access: 70

In Apple Business Manager: 71

Share Calendar, Reminders, and Photos 72

How to Create an Apple ID for Your Child 74

Parental Controls and Restrictions 75

Use Find My 78

Share Media and Apps 78

Share iCloud+ Features 80

Update a Child's Age 81

Change Family Sharing 82

CHAPTER VII: ORGANIZING AND HANDLING YOUR PHOTO LIBRARY 85

iCloud Photos 85

iCloud Shared Photo Library 85

Shared Albums 86

Syncing Your Photos Using iCloud 86

Syncing iCloud Photos Across Your Devices 88

Learn More About iCloud Photos 89

Share Photos, Videos, and Albums --------- 91

Enable Shared Albums --------- 92

Share Photos or Videos Individually: --------- 93

Share Photos from an iOS or iPadOS Device --------- 94

To Share an Album: --------- 95

Creating a New Shared Album --------- 96

Share Albums from Windows --------- 97

Share a Photo Library --------- 99

How to Set Up and Use iCloud Shared Photo Library: --------- 99

CHAPTER VIII: KEEP DOCUMENTS AND APP DATA IN SYNC --------- 102

How to Enable iCloud Drive: --------- 102

Understanding iCloud Drive: --------- 103

Exploring iCloud Drive: --------- 103

Activate iCloud Drive --------- 104

Managing iCloud Drive Settings: --------- 104

Sync Your Desktop and Documents Folders (or Don't) --------- 105

How iCloud Syncs Desktop and Documents Folders: --------- 106

Considerations Before Enabling Sync: --------- 106

How Desktop & Documents Folder Syncing Works --------- 107

Enable Desktop & Documents Folder Syncing --------- 109

Disable Desktop & Documents Folder Syncing --------- 110

Alternative Methods for Syncing Desktop & Documents Without iCloud Drive --------- 112

Optimize Mac Storage --------- 113

Share Files and Folders on a Mac or PC ---------- 115

Share Items on a PC ---------- 121

Use iCloud Drive Within Mac Apps ---------- 122

Use the Files App for iOS or iPadOS ---------- 123

Use iCloud Drive Within iOS and iPadOS Apps ---------- 126

Troubleshoot iCloud Drive ---------- 127

Use In-App Data Syncing ---------- 128

About Optimized Storage ---------- 129

CHAPTER IX: KEEP MAIL, CONTACTS, AND CALENDARS IN SYNC ---------- 131

Work with iCloud Mail ---------- 131

Use Mail Drop ---------- 135

Sync Your Contacts ---------- 136

Seamless Syncing: ---------- 136

Quirks to Note: ---------- 137

Work with Contact Groups ---------- 137

Share Your Contacts with Someone Else ---------- 138

Sync Your Calendars ---------- 139

CHAPTER X: SYNC OTHER ICLOUD DATA ---------- 142

Safari Bookmarks, iCloud Tabs, and Reading List: ---------- 142

Sync Messages ---------- 143

Use Location-Based Reminders ---------- 144

Work with Notes — 145

Sync Data from Other Apps — 146

Use Universal Clipboard — 147

CHAPTER XI: WORK WITH ICLOUD KEYCHAIN — 149

Enable and Configure iCloud Keychain — 150

Enabling iCloud Keychain — 153

Approve Additional Devices: — 155

Use iCloud Keychain in Safari — 156

Managing Multiple Credentials — 158

Autofill Verification Codes — 159

Storing New Passwords: — 160

Storing Credit Card Information: — 162

Using Keychain Access on macOS: — 165

Considerations: — 167

Use the iCloud Website — 168

The Mail Web App — 170

The Contacts Web App — 171

The Photos Web App — 172

The Reminders Web App — 174

The iWork Web Apps — 174

The iCloud Drive Web App — 174

The News Publisher Web App — 175

CHAPTER XII: FIND MY APP --------- 176

Activate Find My --------- 177

Turn on Find My Device --------- 178

Checking Find My Network: --------- 179

Understand Device and Item Locks --------- 180

Deactivate Find My Device --------- 181

CHPATER XIII: FIND YOUR HARDWARE WITH AN APP --------- 182

Find Your Friends --------- 184

Granting Permission to Share Your Location: --------- 185

Understand How iCloud Backup Works --------- 185

What iCloud Backup Includes: --------- 186

Activate and Configure iCloud Backup --------- 187

Restore an iOS or iPadOS Device from a Backup --------- 189

CHAPTER IV: USE ICLOUD ON AN APPLE TV --------- 191

MANAGE YOUR ACCOUNT --------- 194

iCloud Storage: --------- 195

Data Recovery: --------- 195

File Recovery: --------- 196

Change Payment Settings --------- 196

Check and Modify Your Storage Usage --------- 197

Manage Account Recovery --- 198

Decide on Using an Apple ID Recovery Key --- 199

Set Up Account Recovery Contacts --- 200

ICLOUD SECURITY --- 202

The Cruciality of Account Security --- 202

Delving into Data Protection Measures --- 202

Choose Mastering Strong Passwords --- 204

Two-Factor Authentication --- 205

Activation Lock --- 206

Security Key --- 207

Essential Steps for Protecting Your Data --- 208

Advanced Data Protection --- 209

Account Recovery Setup: --- 209

CHAPTER VIII: ICLOUD ALTERNATIVES AND COMPARISONS --- 211

Advantages of iCloud Over Competitors --- 213

Disadvantages of iCloud Compared to Competitors --- 214

CHAPTER IX: FUTURE OF ICLOUD --- 215

CHAPTER I: INTRODUCTION

A Brief History and Evolution of iCloud

In the ever-evolving landscape of technology, cloud services have become an integral part of our digital lives, revolutionizing the way we store, access, and manage data. Among the pioneers in this domain stands iCloud, a groundbreaking platform introduced by Apple Inc. that redefined the concept of seamless synchronization and accessibility across devices.

The story of iCloud finds its roots in Apple's relentless pursuit of simplifying the user experience while ensuring a harmonious connection between their diverse array of products. It's essential to rewind the clock to grasp the foundations upon which iCloud was built.

Predecessors and Early Concepts

Before iCloud's advent, Apple users relied on services like iTools, .Mac, and MobileMe to sync their data across devices. These services, though innovative for their time, were met with certain limitations and complexities. With the launch of iTools in 2000, Apple began its journey into cloud-based services, offering email, online storage, and a suite of internet-based tools.

However, it wasn't until the introduction of .Mac in 2002 that users saw a more integrated approach towards syncing data. .Mac offered features like iDisk for storage, email, and syncing capabilities, laying the groundwork for what would eventually evolve into iCloud.

The Birth of iCloud

The turning point arrived in 2011 when Apple unveiled iCloud at the Worldwide Developers Conference (WWDC). Steve Jobs, Apple's visionary co-founder, introduced this revolutionary service as the successor to MobileMe, emphasizing its ability to seamlessly synchronize content across Apple devices.

iCloud marked a paradigm shift in how users interacted with their data. It aimed to dissolve the barriers between devices, enabling effortless synchronization of photos, music, documents, contacts, and more. With iCloud, users could access their content from anywhere, at any time, providing a unified and consistent experience across their iPhones, iPads, Macs, and even Windows computers.

Core Principles and Functionality

At its core, iCloud was designed to simplify the user experience. Its seamless integration with Apple's ecosystem aimed to eliminate the hassle of manual file transfers or data backups, allowing users to focus on their tasks without worrying about data management.

The service was built on the principles of convenience, security, and synchronization. It offered a suite of features, including iCloud Drive for file storage, iCloud Photos for seamless photo management, iCloud Backup for device backups, iCloud Keychain for password management, and the Find My app for locating lost devices.

Evolution and Iterations

Since its inception, iCloud has undergone iterative improvements and expansions. With each iOS, macOS, or device update, Apple has introduced enhancements to its cloud service, refining its functionalities, improving security measures, and expanding storage options.

The service's growth has been accompanied by a commitment to privacy and security, aligning with Apple's stance on safeguarding user data and ensuring end-to-end encryption across all its services.

Absolutely! Cloud services have become an indispensable part of the modern digital landscape, shaping the way we store, access, and interact with data. Let's explore the significance of cloud services in today's world.

Importance of Cloud Services in Today's Digital World

1. Accessibility and Flexibility

Cloud services have shattered the barriers of physical storage, offering unparalleled accessibility to data from anywhere with an internet connection. This accessibility fosters flexibility, allowing users to work, collaborate, and access their information irrespective of their location or device. Whether it's business documents, personal photos, or collaborative projects, the cloud ensures seamless access across various platforms, including smartphones, tablets, laptops, and desktops.

2. Data Synchronization and Collaboration

One of the most profound advantages of cloud services lies in their ability to synchronize data effortlessly. Whether it's syncing contacts, calendars, or files, the cloud enables real-time updates across multiple devices. This synchronization fosters collaboration by allowing individuals or teams to work concurrently on shared documents, making edits or updates that are instantly reflected across the board. Such collaborative capabilities streamline workflows and enhance productivity in both personal and professional settings.

3. Scalability and Cost Efficiency

Cloud services offer scalability that traditional storage solutions often lack. Users can expand or reduce their storage needs on-demand without the constraints of physical hardware. This scalability also translates to cost efficiency since users only pay for the resources they consume. Small businesses and startups, in particular, benefit from this pay-as-you-go model, as it allows them to scale their operations without significant upfront investments in infrastructure.

4. Disaster Recovery and Data Security

Cloud services provide robust disaster recovery solutions, ensuring data resilience even in the face of hardware failures, natural disasters, or cyber threats. Regular backups and redundancy mechanisms implemented by cloud providers mitigate the risk of data loss. Additionally, reputable cloud services invest heavily in security measures, employing encryption protocols, multi-factor authentication, and continuous monitoring to safeguard sensitive information. These security features instill confidence in users regarding the protection of their data.

5. Innovation and Integration

Cloud services serve as a catalyst for innovation by fostering the development of new applications and services. Developers leverage cloud infrastructure to create and deploy innovative solutions without the burden of managing underlying hardware. Moreover, cloud services seamlessly integrate with various applications and platforms, enabling the convergence of diverse technologies and services. This integration facilitates the creation of interconnected ecosystems that enhance user experiences across different services.

6. Environmental Impact

Cloud services contribute to reducing the environmental footprint associated with traditional IT infrastructure. By consolidating data storage and processing in centralized facilities, cloud providers optimize energy consumption and reduce carbon emissions. Additionally, the shared resources and efficient utilization of server infrastructure by cloud services lead to more sustainable practices in the tech industry.

CHAPTER II: WHAT IS ICLOUD

iCloud stands as Apple's comprehensive cloud-based service designed to seamlessly integrate with its ecosystem of devices, providing users with a unified platform to store, access, and manage their digital content. At its essence, iCloud functions as a centralized hub that synchronizes data across various Apple devices, ensuring a harmonious user experience.

Core Functionalities and Services Offered by iCloud

1. Seamless Data Synchronization:

  - Across Devices: iCloud ensures that data, including photos, contacts, calendars, reminders, and notes, remain updated across all connected Apple devices in real-time. Changes made on one device reflect instantaneously on others, creating a seamless user experience.

2. iCloud Drive:

  - File Storage and Organization: iCloud Drive provides users with a centralized platform to store various file types, including documents, presentations, spreadsheets, images, videos, and more. It offers folder organization and allows for easy management and sharing of files across devices.

  - Collaboration Features: Users can collaborate on documents stored in iCloud Drive, allowing multiple individuals to edit, comment, and work on the same file simultaneously. This feature streamlines teamwork and enhances productivity.

3. iCloud Photos:

- Photo Library: iCloud Photos syncs an entire photo and video library across devices, ensuring that all memories captured on an iPhone or iPad are accessible on other Apple devices. It optimizes storage by storing high-resolution photos and videos in the cloud while providing device-friendly versions to conserve space.

- Organization and Editing: Users can organize their photos into albums, folders, and moments, as well as perform basic editing functions like cropping, filters, and adjustments directly within the Photos app on any synced device.

- Shared Albums: iCloud allows users to create shared albums, enabling them to share specific photos or videos with friends, family, or colleagues and collaborate on a curated collection.

4. iCloud Backup:

- Automatic Device Backups: iCloud Backup automatically backs up essential data from Apple devices, including settings, app data, messages, photos, and more to the cloud. These backups occur when the device is connected to Wi-Fi, ensuring that users have a recent copy of their data in case of device loss or failure.

- Seamless Device Restoration: Users can easily restore data from an iCloud Backup when setting up a new device or restoring an existing one, ensuring a smooth transition without losing critical information.

5. iCloud Keychain:

- Password Management: iCloud Keychain securely stores and syncs passwords, credit card information, and other sensitive data across devices. It generates and stores strong, unique passwords for different accounts and autofills them when needed, enhancing security and convenience.

6. Find My:

- Device Tracking: The Find My app within iCloud allows users to locate and track their Apple devices, even if they are offline. It helps users pinpoint the last known location of a lost or stolen device and offers features like Lost Mode to secure data or remotely wipe the device to prevent unauthorized access.

Absolutely, the system requirements for iCloud vary slightly depending on the device and the services being utilized. Here's a breakdown of the general system requirements for iCloud across various devices and platforms:

System Requirements for iCloud

macOS

- Operating System: iCloud is integrated into macOS versions that support it. Generally, it's available on macOS X Lion (10.7) or later versions.

- App Compatibility: Various iCloud features are integrated into apps like Photos, Contacts, Calendar, Mail, Notes, Safari, and others, making them accessible and synchronized through iCloud.

iPhone, iPad, iPod Touch

- Operating System: iCloud is available on devices running iOS 5 or later. This covers a wide range of devices, but for optimal performance and access to the latest features, running the latest iOS version is recommended.

- App Integration: iCloud syncs data across various native apps on iOS devices, including Photos, Contacts, Calendar, Mail, Notes, Reminders, Safari, and more.

iCloud on Windows PC

- Operating System: iCloud for Windows is compatible with Windows 7 or later.

- App Compatibility: iCloud for Windows allows users to access their iCloud Drive, iCloud Photos, Mail, Contacts, Calendar, and Tasks on their Windows computer. Users can also sync bookmarks with Safari, Internet Explorer, Firefox, or Chrome.

Web Access

iCloud.com

- Browser Compatibility: Users can access some iCloud features via supported web browsers such as Safari, Chrome, Firefox, or Microsoft Edge by visiting iCloud.com. However, certain functionalities might be limited compared to using iCloud through dedicated Apple devices or software.

Storage Plan Requirements

iCloud Storage Plans

- Storage Plans: While iCloud services are available across devices, the amount of free iCloud storage is limited. Additional storage beyond the free allocation can be purchased in various tiers ranging from 50GB to 2TB, allowing users to store more data in the cloud.

CHAPTER III: HOW DOES ICLOUD WORK?

1. Cloud-Based Storage Infrastructure:

iCloud relies on a vast and secure network of servers hosted in data centers worldwide. These data centers store user data across various services, ensuring redundancy and availability. Apple's data centers leverage advanced infrastructure and technologies to maintain the integrity and security of stored data.

2. Synchronization via Push Notifications:

iCloud employs push notifications to facilitate real-time synchronization of data across devices. When changes occur on one device, such as adding a new contact or editing a document, iCloud sends push notifications to other connected devices, prompting them to sync and update the relevant information.

3. CloudKit Framework:

For developers integrating iCloud into their apps, Apple offers the CloudKit framework. This framework provides developers with tools and APIs to access iCloud's storage and syncing capabilities securely. CloudKit handles authentication, data storage, and synchronization, enabling developers to focus on building apps without managing complex server infrastructures.

4. Differential Privacy and Encryption:

To protect user privacy, iCloud employs differential privacy techniques. This approach adds noise to collected data, ensuring anonymity while still providing valuable insights for improving services. Additionally, iCloud uses end-to-end encryption for certain data, ensuring that only authorized users can access and decrypt their information.

5. Content Delivery Network (CDN):

Apple utilizes a Content Delivery Network (CDN) to enhance the performance of iCloud services. The CDN ensures efficient and rapid delivery of content, such as photos, videos, and app data, by caching it closer to the user's geographical location, reducing latency and improving overall user experience.

6. Selective Data Syncing:

iCloud allows selective syncing of data, enabling users to choose which content gets synchronized across their devices. This feature helps optimize storage space on devices by allowing users to control what data is stored locally and what remains primarily in the cloud.

7. Automatic Backup and Restoration:

iCloud's automatic backup feature ensures that users' devices are regularly backed up to the cloud. This process occurs when the device is connected to Wi-Fi, locked, and plugged in. In case of device loss, damage, or upgrade, users can seamlessly restore their data from the latest backup stored in iCloud.

Synchronization Across Apple Devices

1. Unified Apple ID:

  - iCloud synchronization is facilitated through a unified Apple ID associated with all connected devices. This single Apple ID acts as the key to access iCloud services, allowing devices to communicate and sync data.

2. Real-Time Updates:

- Changes made on one device trigger near-instantaneous updates across all other connected devices. For instance, editing a contact, adding a calendar event, or updating a note on one device triggers iCloud to push these changes to other devices, ensuring data consistency.

3. Supported Data Types:

- iCloud synchronizes various types of data, including contacts, calendars, reminders, notes, Safari bookmarks, photos, videos, documents (via iCloud Drive), and app-specific data for apps using iCloud syncing capabilities.

4. Automatic Synchronization:

- iCloud syncs data automatically in the background when devices are connected to Wi-Fi, ensuring that updates occur seamlessly without requiring manual intervention from users.

5. Conflict Resolution:

- In the event of conflicting changes made on different devices to the same piece of data, iCloud employs conflict resolution mechanisms to prioritize the most recent change or prompts the user to choose the preferred version.

6. Optimization for Storage:

- iCloud optimizes storage by managing which content is stored locally on each device and what remains primarily in the cloud. For example, iCloud Photos uses optimization techniques to store lower-resolution versions on devices while retaining high-resolution versions in the cloud, saving device storage space.

7. Developer Integration:

- App developers can leverage iCloud APIs and frameworks, such as CloudKit, to enable synchronization of app-specific data across devices. This integration allows for seamless user experiences within apps and ensures data consistency across platforms

8. Cross-Platform Support:

- iCloud synchronization is not limited to Apple's own devices. While the seamless experience is optimized within the Apple ecosystem, certain iCloud features, such as iCloud.com, enable access to data through supported web browsers on non-Apple devices.

iCloud employs robust data storage and security measures to ensure the safety, integrity, and privacy of user data stored within its ecosystem. Let's delve into the specifics of iCloud's data storage practices and the measures taken to safeguard user information.

Data Storage in iCloud

1. Centralized Cloud Storage:

- iCloud stores user data, including photos, videos, documents, app data, and more, in centralized cloud servers housed within Apple's data centers across different geographical locations.

2. Redundancy and Availability:

- Data stored in iCloud benefits from redundancy measures, where copies of the same data are stored across multiple servers. This redundancy ensures data availability and resilience against hardware failures or data center outages.

3. Efficient Use of Space:

- iCloud optimizes storage space on devices by managing which content is stored locally and which remains primarily in the cloud. For example, iCloud Photos stores high-resolution images and videos in the cloud while providing device-friendly versions to conserve local storage.

4. Selective Data Syncing:

- Users can choose what data gets synchronized across their devices, enabling them to control and optimize storage usage based on their preferences and device capabilities.

Security Measures in iCloud

1. End-to-End Encryption:

- Certain sensitive user data in iCloud, such as iCloud Keychain, iCloud Backup, and end-to-end encrypted data in apps like Messages and Health, is protected by robust encryption protocols. This encryption ensures that only authorized users have access to their data.

2. Differential Privacy:

- iCloud employs differential privacy techniques to gather insights from user data without compromising individual privacy. By adding noise to collected data, Apple ensures the anonymity of user information while still gaining valuable insights for service improvements.

3. Two-Factor Authentication (2FA):

- iCloud offers two-factor authentication as an additional layer of security. 2FA requires users to provide a second form of verification (like a code sent to a trusted device) alongside a password, enhancing the security of iCloud accounts.

4. Continuous Security Updates:

  - Apple regularly updates iCloud's security measures to address emerging threats and vulnerabilities. These updates encompass encryption enhancements, security patches, and privacy-focused improvements to fortify the protection of user data.

5. Transparent Privacy Policies:

  - Apple maintains a commitment to transparency regarding user privacy. The company's privacy policies outline how user data is handled, providing users with insights into how their information is used and protected within iCloud.

iCloud Features and Services

A. iCloud Drive: File Storage and Organization

iCloud Drive serves as a centralized storage hub within iCloud, enabling users to store various file types, organize content efficiently, and access their data seamlessly across Apple devices.

File Storage:

iCloud Drive provides users with storage space in the cloud to save documents, presentations, spreadsheets, images, videos, and more. This storage space is accessible from different Apple devices and via the iCloud website.

Organization:

1. Folder Structure: Users can create folders to organize their files hierarchically. This structure allows for better categorization and easy access to specific sets of documents or media.

2. Drag-and-Drop Functionality: iCloud Drive supports drag-and-drop functionality, enabling users to easily move files between folders or directly upload content from their devices.

3. File Tagging: Users can apply tags to files, enhancing organization and making it simpler to find specific files based on custom tags like "Work," "Personal," "Important," etc.

4. Document Versioning: For certain file types, iCloud Drive maintains multiple versions of documents, enabling users to revert to previous versions if needed, providing an element of document history and recovery.

Collaboration and Sharing:

1. Collaborative Editing: Users can collaborate on documents stored in iCloud Drive in real-time. Multiple users can work on the same document simultaneously, making edits and seeing changes reflected instantly.

2. File Sharing: iCloud Drive facilitates file sharing, allowing users to share files and folders with others via links or specific user invitations. Users can set permissions for view-only or editing access.

CHAPTER IV: HOW TO SETUP

Apple IDs

Using iCloud necessitates an Apple ID, essentially your universal identifier across various Apple services and products. Chances are, you already possess an Apple ID; if not, acquiring one is simple and cost-free.

Initially, Apple allowed any distinct name to function as an Apple ID. Presently, however, they mandate that all Apple IDs must be email addresses. An @icloud.com, @me.com, or @mac.com email denotes an Apple ID. Similarly, if you utilized an alternate email while purchasing from Apple or engaging in various Apple services like the developer program, that email also qualifies as an Apple ID. Uncertain about your Apple ID's existence or if a specific address qualifies? Verify it through the Apple ID "iForgot" site.

While seemingly straightforward, iCloud's reliance on Apple IDs carries nuances. You might possess multiple Apple IDs without knowing which to employ for iCloud, or you could be sharing an Apple ID. Discover how to navigate such scenarios below.

Multiple Apple ID

Having multiple Apple IDs can complicate things. Ideally, one ID would house all your data and purchases, eliminating the need to juggle multiple IDs. But due to various reasons, many people end up with multiple personal Apple IDs.

The main issue with multiple IDs lies in purchases—they're tied permanently to the specific ID used. Transferring purchases between IDs or merging them isn't possible. However, iCloud Family Sharing can alleviate this within a family by linking up to six IDs, allowing access to each other's purchases.

If Family Sharing isn't suitable and you need to share purchases outside your family, there are workarounds. While certain Apple services only permit one ID at a time, you can switch between them without losing content. Simply sign out of one account and sign in with the other, albeit needing the password for each.

Some maintain multiple personal Apple IDs for various reasons—keeping separate iCloud accounts for different purposes like home, work, or different countries they frequent.

Implications of Sharing an Apple ID

If you find yourself sharing an Apple ID with someone else, it's not exactly how Apple intends their system to work. Most iCloud features are designed assuming a single user per Apple ID, so sharing one can lead to various issues. However, despite this, many still opt to share a single account with a spouse, family, or another group.

While some couples prefer sharing everything, including email, the primary reason for shared Apple IDs, apart from purchasing consolidation (which can now be addressed through iCloud Family Sharing), often revolves around contact sharing. To achieve shared contacts without sharing all data, some create an extra iCloud account solely for this purpose, adding it to multiple users' devices.

Handling a shared Apple ID involves creating individual accounts, crucial for maintaining separate settings and avoiding syncing errors or other complications that arise when a shared account becomes each person's primary one. If you only have a shared account, it's advisable to create an individual account when setting up iCloud.

Choosing the Right Apple ID for iCloud Services?

When setting up iCloud, here's a breakdown of which Apple ID to use:

- Single, personal Apple ID: This is the ideal choice—use this one and you're set!

- Single, shared Apple ID: Create a new Apple ID for yourself. Then, add the shared Apple ID as a secondary account in System Settings/System Preferences > Internet Accounts.

- Multiple individual Apple IDs: Opt for the Apple ID linked to your primary or personal account—the one containing most of your data. Later, add secondary iCloud accounts in System Settings/System Preferences > Internet Accounts (or in iOS/iPadOS, Settings > Accounts & Passwords > Add Account) for specific purposes like syncing shared contacts or accessing additional email accounts.

Remember, any iCloud account added after the initial one will have limitations on what it can access on that device. For instance, it can handle email, contacts, calendars, reminders, and notes, but won't access Safari data, iCloud Photos, iCloud Drive, iCloud Keychain, or Find My Device.

For instance, if you aim to share iCloud contacts with your spouse, the best approach involves configuring individual iCloud accounts as primary on each device. Then, set up another iCloud account specifically for contacts, added as a secondary account on each device. While theoretically possible for notes, attempting similar sharing for other data types might not work well or could lead to problems.

Handling different scenarios involving Apple IDs:

- Personal Apple ID and a separate one for shared purchases: It's recommended to solely use your personal Apple ID for iCloud, associating it with your preferred credit card. Then, include other family members in iCloud Family Sharing. If this isn't feasible due to using a business credit card, set up iCloud with your personal Apple ID. Later, in apps like Music, the Mac App Store, or Books/iBooks, sign in with the other Apple ID used for purchases.

- One or more Apple IDs without an iCloud account: When setting up iCloud, your Apple ID will transform into an iCloud account. Enter the Apple ID that has the most purchase history. During this setup, you'll be prompted for additional details, including choosing an email address in the icloud.com domain.

- No Apple ID at all: While this is rare for users of Apple products, if you've never had an Apple ID, you can create one on the "Create Your Apple ID" page via the Apple ID site.

Each scenario requires specific steps to ensure the smooth functioning of your Apple IDs and iCloud services, catering to various needs and purchase histories associated with each ID.

Set Up iCloud

Setting up iCloud is a breeze, especially since it doesn't require any additional software on Mac or iOS/iPadOS devices. Windows, however, may involve a few more steps. While the process is straightforward, you might have queries about specific settings, managing multiple iCloud accounts, or disabling iCloud. In this chapter, I'll guide you through these topics for Macs and iOS/iPadOS devices.

For those who've already set up iCloud, a quick skim through this chapter—starting with "Set Up iCloud on a Mac"—ensures all desired features are enabled.

To make the most of iCloud's latest features, it's crucial to keep your Apple software up to date across all platforms you use:

- iOS/iPadOS: Access Settings > General > Software Update on your devices to install any pending updates.

- Mac: Navigate to Apple ▢> App Store and click Updates. If newer versions of macOS, Photos, or iWork apps (Pages, Numbers, Keynote) are available, follow the prompts to install them. Make sure to get macOS 13 Ventura, a free upgrade, if your Mac supports it and you haven't already updated.

- Windows: Download and install iCloud for Windows from the Microsoft Store.

- Apple TV: For guidance on updating Apple TV software, refer to Apple's article "Update the software on your Apple TV."

By keeping your Apple software up to date, you ensure access to the latest iCloud functionalities and features across your devices.

Set Up iCloud on a Mac

Setting up iCloud on your Mac is a fairly straightforward process. If your Mac hasn't prompted you to set up iCloud yet, here's a guide to help you configure it manually. The steps may differ based on your situation:

1. Access System Settings or System Preferences:

- For macOS Ventura or later: Go to System Settings > Account Name.

  - For macOS Monterey or earlier: Navigate to System Preferences > Apple ID.

  - If you haven't signed in, the pane may be labeled "Sign in."

2. Enter Your Apple ID:

  - Input the Apple ID you want to use and click "Next."

3. Password Entry:

  - Enter your password when prompted and click "Next" again.

4. Potential Prompts You Might Encounter:

  - Agree to the iCloud Terms of Service if they appear.

  - macOS may request reentry of your iCloud password or your Mac's user account password, or both (pay attention to the instructions).

  - You might be asked to allow iCloud to use your Mac's location for Find My Mac.

  - If signing back in after signing out, you may be asked about merging data from apps like Calendar, Safari, and News with iCloud (typically recommended).

  - You might encounter a prompt saying "Update Apple ID Settings." If present, click "Continue" and follow the instructions, which may involve reentering your iCloud and/or Mac's user account password.

5. Accessing iCloud Settings:

- Once you've addressed the alerts, you'll see the full Apple ID pane. If not already selected, click on "iCloud" to view and adjust your iCloud settings. Many services might already be enabled

This guide should help you set up iCloud manually on your Mac, ensuring that your preferred settings are configured to your liking.

6. Manage Types of Data:

To manage the types of data you want with iCloud on your Mac, utilize switches or checkboxes to enable specific features. Click on general categories like iCloud Drive to display controls and configure settings for each feature. Unless you have a particular reason to avoid any, consider enabling all of them for a comprehensive iCloud experience.

If you haven't set up Keychain previously, enabling it involves additional steps beyond toggling its switch or checkbox. If you wish to set it up now, refer to instructions ahead in "Work with iCloud Keychain." Alternatively, you can leave it disabled for the moment and return to it when you're ready. If you previously had Keychain enabled, turned it off, and are re-enabling it now, be prepared for a series of alerts and password prompts.

Once satisfied with your settings, close System Settings/System Preferences. Your Mac is now activated with iCloud. Note that specific features related to the Music app may require additional configuration—refer to "Use iCloud Music Features."

Remember to repeat this iCloud configuration process for any other user accounts on your Mac and for any additional Macs you own. Afterwards, proceed to set up iCloud on your other devices to ensure a synced experience across your Apple ecosystem

Set Up iCloud for Windows

After installing iCloud for Windows, you can swiftly configure it in a few steps:

1. Access iCloud App:

   - If the iCloud app doesn't open automatically, find it in the Start menu and launch it.

2. Sign In to iCloud:

   - If prompted, enter your Apple ID and password, then click "Sign In." If you have two-factor authentication or two-step verification enabled, follow the verification prompts.

3. Enabling Services:

   - Tick the checkboxes next to each service you want to enable. Unless you have specific reasons to avoid any, consider enabling them all.

   - Regarding specific services:

     - Photos: As of November 2022, Microsoft Photos for Windows 11 integrates directly with iCloud Photos. Ensure you're using the latest versions of Windows 11 and the Microsoft Store app. Access the Photos option in iCloud, click its Options button, and enable iCloud Photos. You can also choose to enable Shared Albums to share photos. Refer to "Manage Your Photos" for more details on working with iCloud Photos in Windows.

     - Contacts and Calendars: Syncing these items requires Microsoft Outlook 2016 or later. If you have an older version of Outlook or don't have it installed, these options won't appear in the iCloud app.

However, you can still access this data via a web browser. If you have Outlook 2016 or later, enabling Contacts and Calendars may prompt you for your iCloud password one or more times.

This streamlined setup process allows you to configure iCloud for Windows efficiently, enabling desired services for a synchronized experience across your devices.

Here are the steps to complete the setup for specific iCloud services on Windows:

1. Bookmarks:

   - To sync your iCloud bookmarks, select Bookmarks in the iCloud app.

   - Click the "Install Extension" button for each browser you wish to use (Edge, Chrome, or Firefox). Follow the prompts to install the extensions.

   - After selecting Bookmarks and installing extensions, clicking "Apply" will trigger an alert asking if you want to merge your local bookmarks with those in iCloud. Click "Merge."

2. Passwords:

   - For Edge or Chrome (not Firefox), you can install an extension allowing secure use of iCloud Keychain.

   - Once installed, an iCloud Keychain icon appears in the toolbar. On first use, Apple sends a code to iCloud for Windows to validate the plugin, acting as a second factor.

   - When browsing pages with items to fill in, the iCloud Keychain icon appears. Clicking it initiates a check for matching entries, displaying options if found.

3. Activating Services:

  - After configuring your desired services, click "Apply" to activate them. Simply closing the window without applying changes won't activate the selected services.

  - Depending on your selections, additional windows or processes may open as iCloud completes its setup and data transfer.

4. Closing the iCloud App:

  - Once you've completed setup and activated services, click "Close" in the iCloud app to finalize the setup process.

Now, iCloud is up and running on your Windows system. To utilize iTunes-specific features, refer to "Use iCloud Music Features." This completes the setup of iCloud services on your Windows device.

Set Up iCloud in iOS or iPadOS

On an iOS or iPadOS device, follow these steps:

1. Access Settings:

  - Tap "Settings" and look for "Sign in to your Device." Once signed in, your name will appear here instead.

2. Sign In to your Apple ID:

  - Enter your Apple ID and password, then tap "Sign In." If you use two-factor authentication, follow the prompts to enter your verification code. You might also need to input your device's passcode and respond to alerts in certain situations.

3. Configure iCloud Settings:

   - Tap "iCloud" to reveal detailed settings (Figure 5).

   - Tap on a category name like "Photos" to enable the service and adjust its options. To view a complete list of apps and services, tap "Show All." Toggle the switches for services and apps to sync their data with iCloud. Most might already be enabled (shown by a green switch).

   - Specific points to note:

     - iCloud Photos and Shared Albums: Access "Photos" to manage iCloud Photos and Shared Albums (refer to "Manage Your Photos" for further details).

     - iCloud Backup: To switch your iOS or iPadOS backup to iCloud, turn on "iCloud Backup" (more about iCloud Backup in "Understand How iCloud Backup Works").

     - Passwords and Keychain: Configuring iCloud Keychain might require additional steps. Refer to "Work with iCloud Keychain" for detailed instructions.

     - iCloud+ Services: Features like Private Relay and Hide My Email are part of iCloud+ and require configuration. Find instructions in "Browse the Web Privately and Hide Your Email Address."

     - Home Switch: Enable this to sync settings from the Home app (for smart home products) across your iOS and iPadOS devices.

Continuing with specific settings on iOS or iPadOS devices:

- Health Switch: Enables syncing Health app data with the cloud and across your owned iPhones. Note that Health data doesn't sync with other types of Apple hardware.

- Wallet Switch: Specifically available on iPhone and iPod touch, this syncs wallet items like Apple Pay credit cards, loyalty cards, tickets, and coupons among multiple devices. It's important to note that Wallet itself isn't an iCloud feature and isn't discussed in this context.

- Siri Switch: Allows Siri to share learned information across your devices to enhance its responses.

- iCloud Drive Storage: Check your current storage status for iCloud Drive at the top of the screen. For a detailed breakdown of what's backed up using iCloud Backup or to delete backed-up data for specific apps, tap "Manage Account Storage" or "Manage Storage." Refer to "Activate and Configure iCloud Backup" for further guidance.

Now, iCloud is configured on your iOS or iPadOS device. To utilize iTunes Match or other Music-related features, follow the steps outlined in the next chapter. If you have additional iOS or iPadOS devices, repeat these steps for each one to ensure consistent iCloud settings across your devices.

Work with Multiple iCloud Accounts

Working with multiple iCloud accounts is a scenario I don't assume in this book, as it's typically based on the premise of a single iCloud account per person. However, there are situations where someone might manage more than one active iCloud account, each containing distinct data such as email, contacts, and calendars.

For instance, having a personal account alongside a work account or overseeing an individual work account and a departmental one for monitoring purposes are common scenarios. In these cases, it's possible to set up your Mac or iOS/iPadOS device to access multiple iCloud accounts concurrently, albeit with certain limitations. This technique can also be used to share a set of contacts with a family member or friend, which is covered in "Share Your Contacts with Someone Else" later in this book.

Use Multiple iCloud Accounts on a Mac

On a Mac, individual user accounts can each be linked to a different iCloud account, providing almost the full range of benefits associated with that specific iCloud account. However, there's a notable exception: Find My Mac can only be active for one iCloud account across all user accounts on the Mac. To activate Find My Mac under a different user account, you'll need to deactivate it from the currently active user's account first.

Each user account on a Mac can have a primary iCloud account with complete access to available services. Additionally, secondary iCloud accounts with more limited access can be added. When a user signs in to an iCloud account, it becomes the primary account for that user, enabling access to iCloud Photos, iCloud Drive, iCloud Keychain, and data syncing for Home, News, Safari, Siri, and Stocks. Any additional iCloud account added while logged in to the same user account is considered secondary, allowing use primarily for email, contacts, calendars, and reminders. You can indeed have multiple secondary iCloud accounts.

To add a secondary iCloud account:

- Navigate to System Settings/System Preferences > Internet Accounts.

- Click on iCloud and follow the prompts to sign in and enable desired features for the secondary account.

This configuration allows each user on the Mac to have their own primary iCloud account with extensive access, as well as the option to add secondary accounts with limited functionality, providing flexibility in managing multiple iCloud accounts.

Use Multiple iCloud Accounts on an iOS or iPadOS Device

On an iOS or iPadOS device, similar to a Mac, you can set up more than one iCloud account. However, there are limitations regarding their functionality:

- The first account configured, designated as the primary account, can be utilized for services like Backup, Home, Find My Device, iCloud Drive, iCloud Photos, Keychain, News, Safari, Siri, Stocks, and push email functionality.

- Secondary accounts, while useful for email, contacts, calendars, and reminders, won't support these aforementioned primary functionalities.

To add a secondary iCloud account on your iOS or iPadOS device:

1. For iOS 16/iPadOS 16 or later:

   - Open Settings and navigate to "Mail" > "Accounts."

   - Tap on "iCloud" and follow the on-screen prompts to add the secondary account.

2. For iOS 15/iPadOS 15:

   - Go to Settings and select "Accounts & Passwords" > "Add Account."

   - Tap on "iCloud" and proceed with the prompts to add the secondary account.

This setup allows you to manage multiple iCloud accounts on your iOS or iPadOS device, leveraging the primary account for a broader range of functionalities while utilizing secondary accounts for specific tasks like email, contacts, calendars, and reminders.

Switch Primary and Secondary Accounts

If you've initially set up an iCloud account as a secondary account but later wish to switch it to become the primary account, here's a step-by-step guide:

1. Remove the Secondary Account:

   - Proceed to remove the secondary iCloud account from your device. (Refer to the method to "Remove an iCloud Account."

2. Sign Out of the Primary Account:

   - Sign out of the primary iCloud account currently set as the primary one on your device.

3. Sign In with the Former Secondary Account (New Primary Account):

   - Sign back in with the iCloud account that was previously the secondary account but is now intended to be the primary one.

4. Sign In with the Former Primary Account (New Secondary Account):

   - Now, you can sign back in with the former primary iCloud account that you want to designate as the secondary account.

Following these steps will allow you to transition the iCloud accounts, making the former secondary account the primary one and the former primary account the secondary one on your device. This method can help reassign the functionalities associated with the primary iCloud account to the desired account.

Disable iCloud

Disable Individual Features

On macOS:

- Navigate to System Settings > Account Name > iCloud (Ventura or later) or System Preferences > Apple ID > iCloud (Monterey or earlier).

- Uncheck or turn off the features you no longer wish to use on that particular device.

On Windows:

- Access the iCloud app.

- Within the app, disable the features you want to turn off.

On iOS/iPadOS:

- For iOS 16/iPadOS 16 or later, go to Settings > Mail > Accounts > Account Name > iCloud.

- For iOS 15/iPadOS 15, visit Settings > Accounts & Passwords > Account Name.

Disable Services for a Secondary Account

On macOS:

- Go to System Settings/System Preferences > Internet Accounts.

- Select the secondary iCloud account.

- Disable or uncheck the features you no longer want to use with that secondary account.

On iOS/iPadOS:

- For iOS 16/iPadOS 16 or later, access Settings > Mail > Accounts > Account Name > iCloud.

- For iOS 15/iPadOS 15, visit Settings > Accounts & Passwords > Account Name.

For both primary and secondary accounts, disabling features or services can be done by unchecking or turning off the options you no longer wish to utilize on a specific device. It's important to note that while you may remove data associated with these features from a device, it will still be stored in the cloud. If you re-enable the feature later, the data will be re-downloaded onto the device.

Remove a Device from Find My Device

On macOS:

- Ventura or later (macOS):

  - Go to System Settings > Account Name > iCloud.

  - Toggle off the option for "Find My Device."

- Monterey or earlier (macOS):

  - Navigate to System Preferences > Apple ID > iCloud.

  - Disable "Find My Device" by unchecking the box.

On iOS/iPadOS:

- Go to Settings > Account Name > iCloud.

- Locate "Find My Device" and turn it off.

Additional Notes:

- For iOS/iPadOS Device Erasure:

  - You can also remove a device from Find My Device by erasing it completely.

  - Go to Settings > General > Reset > Erase All Content and Settings.

  - This will erase all data and settings from the device, and it will no longer be associated with your iCloud account in Find My Device.

- For Additional Help:

  - Apple's support article "Remove a device from Find My iPhone on iCloud.com" provides more detailed instructions if needed.

Before buying or selling a used Mac or iOS/iPadOS device, ensure the previous owner has signed out of Find My Device to prevent potential issues. Similarly, if you're selling a device, make sure to sign out before handing it over to avoid complications. Always verify the Activation Lock status to ensure smooth transitions between owners.

Remove an Item from Find My Item

Removing an item from Find My Item involves specific considerations due to the Pairing Lock feature. Here's what you need to know:

Pairing Lock Removal:

- Proximity to Paired Device:

  - Pairing Lock can only be removed when the item (like AirTags, AirPods Pro/Max, or iPhone Leather Wallet) is near the paired iOS/iPadOS device.

- Device Accessibility:

  - Ensure the paired iOS/iPadOS device is accessible to remove the Pairing Lock. If the paired device is lost, stolen, or no longer functional, the item becomes permanently unusable.

- Limitations:

  - Once paired, if the paired device is lost or damaged, the item cannot be re-paired with another device. Apple ID credentials cannot remove Pairing Lock from the item.

Devices Under Pairing Lock:

- Affected Devices:

  - AirTags, AirPods Pro, AirPods Max, and the iPhone Leather Wallet are subject to Pairing Lock.

Removal of Pairing Lock:

- Proximity Required:

  - To remove Pairing Lock, the item must be near the paired iOS/iPadOS device. Without this proximity, the lock cannot be removed.

Apple's Note:

- Permanent Unusability:

  - If the paired device is lost, stolen, or no longer accessible, the item becomes permanently unusable and cannot be paired with another device.

Apple has implemented Pairing Lock as a security measure to protect these devices. It's crucial to maintain access to the paired device to manage and remove Pairing Lock for these Find My Item devices.

CHAPTER V: HOW TO USE ICLOUD+

Setting Up iCloud+

Setting up iCloud+ is an essential initial step to harness its features and functionalities across your Apple devices. The setup process ensures seamless integration and access to enhanced services within the iCloud ecosystem.

Steps to Set Up iCloud+:

1. Device Sign-In:

   - Ensure you are signed in to your Apple ID on your iPhone, iPad, Mac, or other compatible Apple devices.

2. Access iCloud Settings:

   - iOS/iPadOS Devices:

     - Open "Settings."

     - Tap your Apple ID profile.

     - Select "iCloud" and then choose "Upgrade to iCloud+."

   - Mac:

     - Navigate to "System Preferences."

     - Click on "Apple ID."

- Choose "iCloud" from the sidebar and select "Upgrade to iCloud+."

3. Select a Plan:

   - Review the available iCloud+ plans offering increased storage and enhanced features.

   - Choose a plan that suits your storage needs and budget.

   - Follow the prompts to complete the subscription process.

4. Enable Enhanced Features:

   - Once subscribed to iCloud+, explore and enable enhanced features like iCloud Private Relay, Hide My Email, and other privacy-focused functionalities.

   - Customize settings to optimize privacy and security preferences according to your requirements.

5. Verify Across Devices:

   - Ensure that all your connected Apple devices, such as iPhones, iPads, Macs, and others, are also signed in with the same Apple ID to access iCloud+ features across your ecosystem.

6. Data Migration (if needed):

   - If migrating from a previous iCloud plan or another cloud service, initiate data transfers or backups to ensure a smooth transition to iCloud+.

7. Confirmation and Acknowledgment:

   - Once set up, review the confirmation of your iCloud+ subscription and familiarize yourself with the upgraded features and additional storage allocation.

iCloud+ represents an expanded suite of services beyond basic storage and synchronization. Here's what iCloud+ encompasses:

Features Included in iCloud+ Tiers:

1. Storage and Sync:

   - Includes the fundamental storage and synchronization functions that iCloud originally offered.

2. Privacy Enhancements:

   - Hide My Email:

     - Generate unique, random email addresses to prevent sharing your personal email.

   - Private Relay (VPN-like feature):

     - Encrypts browsing activities and disguises the user's IP address for added privacy.

3. Enhanced Security:

   - iCloud Keychain:

     - Securely stores passwords, credit card information, and other sensitive data.

4. HomeKit Secure Video:

   - Allows storage and analysis of security camera footage directly within iCloud.

5. Expanded Services:

   - Additional Cameras (Varies by Tier):

- The number of cameras supported by HomeKit Secure Video varies depending on the specific tier of iCloud+.

Tier Variations:

- Uniform Features:

  - All iCloud+ tiers offer the same set of services, except for the camera limitations in HomeKit Secure Video, which vary based on the chosen tier.

iCloud vs. iCloud+:

- Differentiation:

  - The free tier with 5 GB of storage and synchronization is referred to as "iCloud."

  - Any paid tier, including the expanded services and additional features, falls under the umbrella term "iCloud+."

Maximizing Storage Capacity

Expanding your storage with iCloud+ offers various options depending on your needs and can be managed easily through your devices. Here's how you can increase your storage:

Mac or PC:

1. Access Settings:

   - Navigate to System Settings > Account Name > iCloud (Ventura or later) or System Preferences > Apple ID > iCloud (Monterey or earlier) on Mac, or use the iCloud app on Windows.

2. Enter Storage Management:

   - Click the Manage button (Mac) or Storage (Windows) near the iCloud Storage indicator.

3. Purchase More Storage:

   - Click on "Change Storage Plan" (if you have an existing paid plan and wish to upgrade) or "Add Storage/Buy More Storage" (if not subscribed yet).

4. Select Desired Plan:

   - Choose the storage plan that suits your needs from the options available (50 GB, 200 GB, 1 TB, etc.).

5. Complete Purchase:

   - Enter your password when prompted and proceed to buy the selected plan.

iOS or iPadOS Device:

1. Access Settings:

   - Tap Settings > Account Name > iCloud > Manage Account Storage (or Manage Storage).

2. Purchase More Storage:

   - Tap "Change Storage Plan" (if you have an existing paid plan and wish to upgrade) or "Add Storage/Buy More Storage" (if not subscribed yet).

3. Select Desired Plan:

   - Choose the storage plan that suits your needs from the available options.

4. Confirm Purchase:

   - Confirm your selection and complete the purchase when prompted.

Automatic Renewal:

- Subscription Renewal:

   - Any additional storage purchased will automatically renew monthly unless canceled before the renewal date.

Family Sharing:

- Sharing Option:

   - Family Sharing users can share the purchased storage with other family members, making it beneficial for the whole family.

By following these steps, you can easily increase your iCloud+ storage based on your requirements, and the subscription will renew each month unless manually canceled before the renewal date.

Exploring Private Web Browsing

iCloud Private Relay is a smart feature that offers a layer of privacy when you're surfing the web. Here's a breakdown of how it works:

The Two-Server System:

- Apple's Server: Acts as the initial stop for your browsing requests.

- Third-Party Partner's Server: Apple collaborates with a few trusted partners who run the second server.

Encryption and Data Handling:

- Safari's Encryption: When using Private Relay, Safari encrypts your requests before sending them to Apple's server.

- Apple's Action: Upon receiving the request, Apple removes the location data and forwards it to the third-party server.

- Third-Party Server's Role: It decrypts the request, selects an IP address not linked to you, and sends the query to the intended website.

- Response Encryption: The server encrypts the website's response and relays it back through Apple's server to your Safari browser.

Maintaining Anonymity:

- Secured Data Transfer: This two-step process ensures that neither Apple nor the third-party server has complete information about your browsing activity.

- Your Privacy Control: You have the choice to configure the IP address's geographical association, providing a level of anonymity based on your preference.

Additional Protection:

- Expanding Security: Private Relay extends its protection to DNS lookups and insecure HTTP requests across all apps and services on your device.

- Enhanced Privacy: By safeguarding DNS lookups, it shields the translation of human-readable addresses into machine-readable ones.

By using iCloud Private Relay, you're adding a layer of privacy to your browsing experience. It obscures your location from websites, making it harder for them to gather personal information without your explicit input.

Activating and Customizing iCloud Private Relay

Enabling and fine-tuning iCloud Private Relay settings for added privacy is simple once you locate the right options:

On iOS/iPadOS:

- Settings Path: Settings > Account Name > iCloud > Private Relay

- Enable Private Relay: Tap the Private Relay option to turn it on and access additional settings.

On macOS:

- Settings Path (Ventura or Later): System Settings > Account Name > iCloud > Private Relay

- Settings Path (Monterey or Earlier): System Preferences > Apple ID > iCloud

- Configuration Steps:

  - Click on Private Relay (Ventura or later) or check the Private Relay box and click Options (Monterey or earlier).

- Adjust Location Coarseness: Choose between "Maintain general location" or "Use country and time zone" for varying degrees of location privacy.

Disabling iCloud Private Relay:

- iOS/iPadOS/MacOS: Reverse the enabling steps, toggling off Private Relay or selecting the "Turn Off" option in settings.

Advanced Configuration (Ventura and iOS 16/iPadOS 16):

- Disabling for Individual Webpages in Safari:

  - macOS: Choose View > Reload and Show IP Address in Safari.

  - iOS/iPadOS: Tap the AA icon in the address bar and choose "Show IP Address" from the pop-up menu.

These settings allow you to control the level of anonymity when browsing online. Disabling Private Relay for specific webpages in Safari can resolve any issues with loading or accessing content when the feature is enabled.

Hide Your Email Address

Apple's Hide My Email service within iCloud+ is designed to enhance user privacy and limit exposure of personal email addresses when interacting with websites or making purchases. Here's how you can use Hide My Email across different Apple devices:

On macOS:

- Ventura or Later: System Settings > Account Name > iCloud > Hide My Email

- Monterey or Earlier: System Preferences > Apple ID > iCloud > Hide My Email

- Click on "Options" next to Hide My Email, then use the plus icon to create a new alias.

On iOS/iPadOS (15 or later):

- Settings Path: Settings > Account Name > iCloud > Hide My Email

- Tap "Create new address" to generate a new alias for your iCloud account.

On iCloud Website:

- Accessing Hide My Email: Click the menu icon at the top and select "Hide My Email."

- Click the plus icon to add a new email alias to your iCloud account.

With Hide My Email, you can effortlessly create custom, random email addresses to use with various websites or services. Emails sent to these generated addresses will be forwarded to your iCloud account, keeping your real email address hidden from the sender. Additionally, you have the flexibility to deactivate these aliases at any time for added control over your digital footprint.

The Hide My Email service offers several convenient functionalities across various Apple devices, allowing users to manage and utilize generated email aliases effectively:

Editing Existing Entries:

- Copy Address: Select an existing entry to copy its associated public address.

- Change Label or Note: Modify the Label or Note to customize the alias's display name or add a description.

- Deactivate: Stop mail forwarding for an alias by deactivating it.

Changing Forwarding Address:

- iOS/iPadOS: Scroll to the bottom, tap "Forward to," select an address, and tap Done.

- macOS Ventura or Later: Click the settings icon, choose "Change Forwarding Address," select an address, and click Done.

- macOS Monterey or Earlier: Click "Options" next to Forward To and select an address.

- iCloud Website: Choose a different radio button under "Forward to."

Mail App Integration:

- Composing an Email: Within the Mail app, click the "From:" field while composing a message and choose "Hide My Email" as the option. The Mail app will automatically fill in the generated email alias.

Using the Mail app integration simplifies the process by enabling users to select the Hide My Email alias directly while composing an email. This entry appears instantly in the Hide My Email list across all associated iCloud locations for convenient management.

Setting Up a Custom Domain:

Setting up a custom domain for iCloud Mail involves a few key steps:

Prerequisites:

- Two-Factor Authentication: Ensure it's enabled for your Apple ID and other members of your Family Sharing group intending to use the custom domain.

- Primary Email Address: Set up a primary email address for iCloud Mail.

Steps to Prepare:

1. Compile Email Addresses: Create a list of all incoming email addresses associated with the custom domain. These addresses will redirect to iCloud Mail once configured.

Steps to Set Up the Custom Domain:

1. Access iCloud Settings:

   - macOS Ventura or Later: Go to System Settings > Account Name > iCloud > Custom Domain.

   - macOS Monterey or Earlier: Navigate to System Preferences > Apple ID > iCloud and click Options next to Custom Domain.

   - iCloud Website: Visit the iCloud website and access Custom Domain settings.

2. Begin Setup:

   - Choose "Add a Custom Domain" or similar.

   - Enter your domain name when prompted.

3. Verification Process:

   - Follow the prompts to verify ownership of the domain. This typically involves adding a TXT or CNAME record in your domain's DNS settings.

4. Email Configuration:

- Configure MX records: Point the domain's MX (Mail Exchange) records to iCloud's mail servers. Apple will provide specific MX record details during the setup process.

5. Adding Email Addresses:

- Add the previously compiled list of email addresses associated with your domain to iCloud Mail.

6. Finalize Setup:

- Confirm completion of the setup and test email functionality to ensure proper forwarding and reception.

Ensure that all necessary settings and verifications are correctly completed before finalizing the domain setup with iCloud Mail. This process will transition the designated email addresses to iCloud Mail servers, allowing you to send and receive emails using your custom domain via iCloud services.

CHAPTER VI: USE ICLOUD FAMILY SHARING

Family Sharing is a fantastic feature for households that want to share purchases, manage subscriptions, and ensure parental controls across Apple devices for up to six family members. Here's a rundown of its features:

1. Consolidated Purchases:

   - All purchases from Apple's ecosystem (apps, media, etc.) are billed to the family organizer's credit card, except when family members use their own credit.

2. Parental Controls:

   - Parents can approve or deny media purchase requests from their kids.

   - Special Apple IDs for kids under 13 can be created.

3. Shared Media Access:

   - Family members have access to each other's purchased media.

   - Customizable sharing allows hiding specific items from being shared.

4. App and Subscription Sharing:

   - Family members can download and use apps, in-app purchases, and subscriptions from other members if sharing is enabled.

5. Shared Digital Assets:

- iCloud automatically generates a shared family photo album, calendar, and reminder list, which can be used as desired.

6. Device Location Sharing:

    - Easier sharing of locations and locating family devices using Find My.

7. Group Apple Music Subscription:

    - A family can join Apple Music for a flat rate, making it more cost-effective than individual subscriptions.

8. Shared Subscriptions with Apple One:

    - With an Apple One subscription at the Family or Premier level, all subscriptions are shared among family members.

9. Shared iCloud+ Features:

    - Family organizer's iCloud+ subscription can be shared among family members, providing access to iCloud Private Relay and Hide My Email.

10. Parental Controls on Screen Time:

    - Parents can manage and limit their kids' screen time on iOS/iPadOS devices and Macs.

These features facilitate a cohesive and controlled digital experience for the family, allowing sharing of media, subscriptions, and device access while maintaining parental oversight and cost efficiency.

Enable Family Sharing

Enabling Family Sharing on your Mac is a seamless process. Here's a step-by-step guide:

1. Access Family Sharing Setup:

   - On a Mac running Ventura or later, navigate to System Settings > Family. For Monterey or earlier versions, head to System Preferences > Family Sharing and click "Next."

2. Confirm Apple ID and Preferences:

   - Follow the prompts and confirm the displayed Apple ID as the organizer.

   - Choose to share purchases, agree to terms and conditions, and understand the billing method (credit card associated with your Apple ID).

3. Location Sharing:

   - Opt to share your location with family members if desired, then click "Continue."

4. Add Family Members:

   - To add adults or children with existing Apple IDs:

     - Select "Enter a family member's name, email address or Game Center nickname."

     - Enter the name or email address and proceed with the prompts.

     - Each invited family member must verify either through your computer or via email invitation.

5. Add Children Without Apple IDs:

   - For children without existing Apple IDs:

- Choose "Create an Apple ID for a child who doesn't have an account."

  - Follow the prompts and create an Apple ID for the child. It will also become their email address.

  - If the chosen Apple ID is unavailable, continue trying until you find an available one.

6. Add Additional Members:

  - To add more family members, click the plus icon and repeat the above process.

7. Completion:

  - Once all members are added, click "Done" to complete the setup.

This process ensures that your family members are linked under Family Sharing, allowing easy sharing of purchases, media, subscriptions, and other benefits across Apple devices.

Setting Up Apps and Services

Here's how to access and modify Family Sharing settings on macOS Ventura or later, and iOS 16/iPadOS 16 or later:

macOS Ventura or later:

1. Access Family Settings:

  - Go to System Settings > Family.

2. Adjust Family Member Settings:

  - To manage individual family member settings:

- Click on a family member's name, then navigate through the categories to modify their services and preferences.

3. Add a Family Member:

   - To include a new family member:

   - Click the "Add Member" option or the People icon to initiate the process.

4. View Subscriptions:

   - Check existing subscriptions:

   - Click on "Subscriptions" to view details about current subscriptions, shared app subscriptions, additional storage, and Apple One features.

5. Manage Purchase Sharing:

   - Review and control purchase sharing:

   - Click on "Purchase Sharing" to monitor shared purchases or to disable this feature if necessary.

6. Location Sharing:

   - Enable or disable location sharing:

   - Click on "Location Sharing" to adjust location sharing settings for each family member.

iOS 16/iPadOS 16 or later:

1. Access Family Settings:

   - Go to Settings > Family.

2. Modify Family Member Settings:

   - Tap on a family member's name to navigate and adjust their specific services and settings.

3. Add a Family Member:

   - Tap "Add Member" or the People icon to invite a new member to the family group.

4. View Subscriptions:

   - Check existing subscriptions:

   - Tap on "Subscriptions" to review and manage current subscriptions, shared app subscriptions, Apple One features, and additional storage.

5. Manage Purchase Sharing:

   - Control purchase sharing:

   - Tap on "Purchase Sharing" to oversee shared purchases or to disable this feature.

6. Location Sharing:

   - Adjust location sharing settings:

   - Tap on "Location Sharing" to enable or disable location sharing for individual family members.

These settings provide detailed control and customization options for your Family Sharing group, ensuring everyone enjoys the benefits in a manner that suits their preferences.

A Guide to Apple School Manager Customizations

Unlock the potential for users to seamlessly access various Apple apps and services while wielding the power of Apple School Manager. As an Administrator, Site Manager, or People Manager, you hold the reins to tailor user access to specific apps and services. With this capability, you can enable or restrict access to a spectrum of features, from iCloud functionalities to FaceTime and iMessage.

Customization knows no bounds. You can designate which users gain access to particular apps and services, extend control over device sign-ins, and fine-tune their privacy and security settings.

Essentials:

To maximize these capabilities, ensure your systems meet these requirements:

- iOS 17, iPadOS 17, macOS 14, or later.

- Seamless integration with your third-party MDM solution. Refer to your MDM vendor's documentation to confirm feature support.

Manage iCloud Features and App Access:

Take charge of the following features to align with your organizational needs, including device-specific sign-ins with Managed Apple IDs:

1. iCloud Storage Options:

   - Off: Prohibit data storage in iCloud.

- Any Device: Enable iCloud data access across various devices.

- Managed Devices Only: Exclusive access limited to devices managed by an MDM solution supporting the new Get Token endpoint.

- Supervised Devices Only: Restricted access, requiring device supervision by an MDM solution supporting the new Get Token endpoint.

Note: iOS 17, iPadOS 17, macOS 14, and MDM support are prerequisites for this feature.

In Apple School Manager:

1. Log in using an account holding the roles of Administrator, Site Manager, or People Manager.

2. Navigate to Access Management in the sidebar, then select Apple Services.

3. iCloud Selection:

   - Define Managed Apple ID sign-in permissions:

     - Off

     - Any Device (default)

     - Managed Devices Only

     - Supervised Devices Only

4. Collaboration Settings:

   - Enable collaboration on Keynote, Numbers, and Pages files, and set preferences for automatic file acceptance:

- Anyone (default): Allow collaboration with any Apple ID users.

- Organization Only: Limit collaboration to users with Managed Apple IDs within the same organization.

- Off: Disable sharing of Keynote, Numbers, or Pages documents.

- Auto Accept Files: Streamline acceptance of collaboration invitations.

- Shared by anyone except students

- Shared by anyone

- Off

5. iCloud Settings:

  - Control access to iCloud features:

    - iCloud Drive

    - Passcodes and Keychain

    - Access to iCloud data on the web

    - iCloud Backup

A Guide to Apple Business Manager Customizations

Empower users with Managed Apple IDs to harness a range of Apple apps and services, all within your control through Apple Business Manager. As an Administrator or People Manager, you wield the authority to curate user access, tailoring it to specific apps and services. Whether enabling selective iCloud features, determining cloud-stored app data, or managing FaceTime and iMessage access, the power rests in your hands.

For further customization, you hold the reins on device-specific sign-ins and can fine-tune privacy and security features.

System Requirements:

To unlock these capabilities, ensure your systems meet the following prerequisites:

- iOS 17, iPadOS 17, macOS 14, or newer.

- Seamless integration with your third-party MDM solution. Check your MDM vendor's documentation for feature support.

Accessing Services with Managed Apple IDs:

Access to specific services may vary while utilizing Managed Apple IDs.

Managing iCloud Features and App Access:

Tailor these features to align with your organizational needs, including control over device sign-ins using Managed Apple IDs:

1. iCloud Storage Options:

   - Off: Prevent data storage in iCloud.

   - Any Device: Enable iCloud data access across various devices.

- Managed Devices Only: Exclusive access limited to devices managed by an MDM solution supporting the new Get Token endpoint.

- Supervised Devices Only: Restricted access, requiring device supervision by an MDM solution supporting the new Get Token endpoint.

Note: This feature requires iOS 17, iPadOS 17, macOS 14, and support from your MDM solution.

In Apple Business Manager:

1. Log in using an account with Administrator or People Manager roles.

2. Navigate to Access Management in the sidebar, then select Apple Services.

3. iCloud Settings:

  - Define Managed Apple ID sign-in permissions:

    - Off

    - Any Device (default)

    - Managed Devices Only

    - Supervised Devices Only

4. Collaboration Settings:

  - Enable collaboration on Keynote, Numbers, and Pages files, and set preferences for automatic file acceptance:

    - Anyone (default): Allow collaboration with any Apple ID users.

- Organization Only: Limit collaboration to users with Managed Apple IDs within the same Apple Business Manager organization.

   - Off: Disable sharing of Keynote, Numbers, or Pages documents.

   - Auto Accept Files: Streamline acceptance of collaboration invitations.

5. iCloud Features:

   - Control access to specific iCloud features:

     - iCloud Drive

     - Passcodes and Keychain

     - Access to iCloud data via www.icloud.com

     - iCloud Backup

Share Calendar, Reminders, and Photos

Apple's Family Sharing makes it easy to sync certain services among family members. Here's a breakdown of how it integrates with Calendar, Reminders, and Photos:

Calendar and Reminders:

- Family Sharing automatically generates a shared Family calendar in the Calendar app and a Family reminder list in the Reminders app.

- Each family member has access to these shared lists and calendars across all their linked devices, including the iCloud web apps.

- Any events or reminders created and assigned to the Family calendar or list will be visible to all family members, ensuring everyone stays informed and updated.

Photos:

- With Family Sharing, a shared photo album called "Family" is created on all devices linked to the family group.

- Users can add photos to this shared album just like any other album, making these images accessible to every family member.

- While the Family album is available for shared photos, managing it might be somewhat complex. For a more streamlined approach, consider sharing an entire photo library, which is a distinct feature from Family Sharing. Check out "Share a Photo Library" for more details on this feature.

By utilizing these shared services, families can maintain synchronized calendars, reminders, and photos, ensuring everyone remains connected and engaged with shared events, tasks, and memorable moments.

Creating an Apple ID for Your Child

Instead of sharing your personal Apple ID with your child, which may lead to unintended access to your private information, consider creating a separate Apple ID for them. This enables you to implement age-appropriate parental controls while allowing your child to utilize Family Sharing, Messages, the App Store, and other Apple services in a safe and monitored manner.

How to Create an Apple ID for Your Child

For children under 13 (age may vary by region), as a family organizer or guardian, you have the ability to set up an Apple ID for your child. Follow these steps based on your device and operating system:

On iPhone, iPad, or iPod touch:

For iOS 16 or iPadOS 16 and later:

1. Go to Settings > Family.
2. Tap the Add Member button, then select Create Child Account and Continue.
3. Enter the child's accurate name and birth date, ensuring it's correct as it can't be modified later.
4. Follow the onscreen prompts to complete the setup. You can use their email address, the suggested @icloud.com address, or their Game Center nickname for your child's Apple ID.

For iOS 15 or earlier:

1. Navigate to Settings.
2. Tap your name, then select Family Sharing.
3. Tap Add Member, choose Create an Account for a Child, and Continue.
4. Proceed with the setup by entering the child's details, including their email address or Game Center nickname, and their correct birth date.

On Mac:

1. For macOS Ventura or later:
1. Choose Apple menu > System Settings and click Family.

2. Click Add Member and select Create Child Account.

3. Complete the setup, entering the child's accurate birth date and selecting an email address or Game Center nickname for their Apple ID.

For macOS Monterey or earlier:

1. Choose Apple menu □> System Preferences and click Family Sharing.

2. Click the Add button and choose Create Child Account.

3. Follow the prompts, providing the child's details and ensuring the correct birth date is entered for their Apple ID.

By creating a dedicated Apple ID for your child, you enable a safer and more controlled experience while granting access to Apple's suite of services."

Parental Controls and Restrictions

Parental controls and restrictions within iCloud Family Sharing empower parents to manage and monitor their children's activities across Apple devices. Implementing these controls ensures a safer and more controlled digital experience for younger users.

1. Adding Child Accounts:

   - Initiating Child Account Creation:

     - Access "Family Sharing" in Settings or System Preferences.

     - Select "Add Family Member" and choose "Create Child Account."

   - Account Setup and Verification:

- Follow the prompts to create a child account, including setting up an Apple ID for the child.

   - Parental consent and verification may be required based on local regulations.

2. Enabling Parental Controls:

   - Screen Time Settings:

     - Access "Screen Time" in Settings.

     - Set up limits for app usage, device usage, and content restrictions suitable for the child's age.

   - Content & Privacy Restrictions:

     - Access "Content & Privacy Restrictions" in Settings.

     - Customize settings for apps, content, and privacy controls, including blocking inappropriate content, controlling app downloads, and limiting explicit content.

3. Managing App Usage and Purchases:

   - Approving App Downloads:

     - Enable "Ask to Buy" for child accounts, allowing parents to approve or decline app downloads and purchases initiated by the child.

   - Family Sharing for Purchases:

     - Ensure that shared purchases and subscriptions through Family Sharing adhere to parental restrictions and controls.

4. Location Sharing and Safety Features:

- Find My Settings:

  - Access "Find My" in Settings.

  - Enable location sharing and set up location-based notifications for added safety and monitoring.

5. Communication Controls:

  - Communications Limits:

  - Utilize "Communication Limits" to manage contacts, messages, and FaceTime for child accounts.

  - Customize who the child can communicate with and when.

6. Monitoring and Reports:

  - Screen Time Reports:

  - View Screen Time reports to monitor the child's device usage and set specific time limits for various activities.

  - Usage Reports and Alerts:

  - Receive alerts or usage reports to stay informed about the child's activities and address any concerns proactively.

Use Find My

Enabling Family Sharing simplifies the use of Find My among family members. Here's what it offers:

1. People View: This feature tracks family members based on their primary device, be it an iPhone, iPad, cellular Watch, or even an iPod touch.

2. Devices View: This view displays the locations of all Apple devices belonging to a family member that have Find My Device activated. It includes iPhones, iPads, iPod touches, Macs, Apple Watches, sets of AirPods or AirPods Pro, AirPods Max headphones, and Beats audio devices.

While you can control and disable location sharing in the People view with family members, turning off device location tracking for the entire family group also disables it for yourself. For a comprehensive guide on managing location sharing and device tracking preferences, refer to the section "Find My Nouns."

Additionally, family members' devices can also be viewed in the Find My web app. (Apple discontinued a separate Find My Friends web app dedicated solely to viewing people's locations in 2021.)

Share Media and Apps

Family Sharing simplifies sharing purchased media and most apps among family members. Here's how you can access and download another family member's purchases across various Apple devices:

Mac Apps:

- App Store app on Mac: Click your name in the sidebar, then choose a family member's name from the "Purchased by" pop-up menu in the upper-right corner.

iOS/iPadOS Apps:

- App Store app on iPhone or iPad: Tap your picture at the top of the screen, select Purchased, then tap a family member's name.

Books:

- Books for Mac: Navigate to Store > Book Store Home and click the Purchased link. Choose a family member's name from the pop-up menu next to Purchased at the top.
- Books for iOS/iPadOS: Tap Reading Now, then tap your picture in the upper-right corner, and select a family member's name.

Music, TV Shows, and Movies:

- Music app (Mac) or iTunes (Windows): Choose Account > Family Purchases, then pick a family member's name from the pop-up menu next to Purchased at the top.
- iTunes Store app (iOS/iPadOS): Open iTunes Store, go to More > Purchased (iPhone) or Purchased > My Purchases (iPad), and select a family member's name.
- Apple TV: Navigate to Movies > Purchased > Family Sharing or TV Shows > Purchased > Family Sharing, and choose a family member's name.

This streamlined access allows family members to enjoy each other's purchased content, facilitating shared access to media and apps.

Share iCloud+ Features

iCloud+ users (including those with an Apple One subscription at the Family or Premier tier) can share their extra storage space, along with Private Relay, Hide My Email, Custom Email Domain, and HomeKit Secure Video, with members of their Family Sharing group.

To share iCloud+ features as the family organizer:

macOS Ventura or later: Go to System Settings > Family > Subscriptions, click iCloud+ under Available to Share, and click Share with Family.

macOS Monterey or earlier: Go to System Preferences > Family Sharing > iCloud Storage, click Share, and follow the prompts.

iOS/iPadOS: In iOS 16/iPadOS 16, go to Settings > Family > Subscriptions > iCloud+; or in iOS 15/iPadOS 15, go to Settings > Account Name > Family Sharing > iCloud+. Then follow the prompts. (If you have another family member who's already paying for storage, you can optionally tap Send Invitation to invite them to switch to your plan.)

Other family members on the free 5 GB storage tier can immediately use the shared space, while family members with their own paid plans can choose to use the shared space or to continue paying for their own.

If they choose to use your shared space, they can follow the instructions they receive (if you invited them using iOS or iPadOS). Or, on a Mac running Ventura or later, they can go to System Settings > Family > Subscriptions > iCloud+ and click Use Shared Plan; on a Mac running Monterey or earlier, they can go to System Preferences > Family Sharing > iCloud Storage and click Use Family Storage.

Update a Child's Age

Absolutely, ensuring accurate details in your child's Apple ID is important. Updating their birthdate in their Apple ID can be done through these steps:

1. Log in to the Child's Apple ID Account:

   - Visit the Apple ID website and log in using the child's Apple ID credentials.

2. Access Personal Information:

- Click on "Personal Information" in the left-hand navigation menu.

3. Modify Birthday:

   - Select the "Birthday" option.

   - Enter the correct birthdate for the child.

4. Save the Changes:

   - Click on "Save" to confirm the new birthdate.

5. Request for Parental Consent:

   - A notification requesting parental consent will appear. This requires approval from the Family Sharing organizer.

6. Approval Process:

   - Apple sends an email to the iCloud account of the Family Sharing organizer, titled "Update Person's birth date?"

   - Open the email and click on "Approve Request" to proceed.

7. Verify and Confirm:

   - The link directs you to a page on the Apple ID site for parental approval.

   - Log in with the organizer's Apple ID credentials if prompted.

   - Review and verify the new birthdate.

   - Apple sends a verification code to all devices linked to the organizer's Apple ID.

- Enter the received code to proceed.

- Agree to the terms to confirm the birthdate change.

This process ensures the accurate representation of the child's age within their Apple ID account.

Change Family Sharing

Certainly, managing Family Sharing and making changes to accommodate evolving family dynamics or other circumstances can be important. Here's an overview of what you can and cannot do in terms of Family Sharing changes:

What You Can Do:

1. Add and Remove Adults:

   - You have the flexibility to add or remove adult family members.

2. Add Children of Any Age:

   - You can add children to the Family Sharing group, regardless of their age.

3. Remove Children Who Have Reached the Cutoff Age:

   - If a child reaches the age cutoff set by Apple (usually 13 or over in many countries), you can remove them from the Family Sharing group.

4. Move Children Below the Cutoff Age to Other Groups:

   - Children below the age cutoff can be moved to other Family Sharing groups if needed.

5. Disband the Family Group (If No Children Below the Cutoff Age):

- If the family group does not contain children below the age cutoff, you can disband the group.

What You Can't Do:

1. Change the Organizer of the Family Sharing Group:

   - The family organizer cannot be changed directly.

2. Disband the Family Group If It Contains Children Below the Cutoff Age:

   - If there are children below the age cutoff in the family group, you cannot disband it.

Workarounds:

1. Changing the Organizer:

   - The direct change of the organizer is not allowed, but you can create a new Family Sharing group with a new organizer and invite existing members.

2. Disbanding With Children Below the Cutoff Age:

   - Move children to another Family Sharing group and then disband the group.

Understanding these capabilities and limitations can help you plan and make adjustments to Family Sharing as needed. Always consider the age restrictions imposed by Apple when making changes involving children.

CHAPTER VII: ORGANIZING AND HANDLING YOUR PHOTO LIBRARY

Using iCloud Photos, iCloud Shared Photo Library, and Shared Albums offers great flexibility in managing your photos across devices and sharing them with others. Here's a breakdown of each feature:

iCloud Photos

- Syncs Across Devices: Keeps your entire Photos library in sync across all your Apple devices.
- Cloud Storage: Photos and videos synced through iCloud Photos count against your iCloud or iCloud+ storage quota.
- Automatic Sync: Changes made to photos or videos on one device reflect across all devices connected to the same iCloud account.
- Convenient Access: Easily access and manage your photos and videos on any Apple device linked to your iCloud account.

iCloud Shared Photo Library

- Sharing with a Small Group: Share a library with a small group of up to six people, including yourself.
- Storage Allocation: The contents of the shared photo library count against the storage of the person sharing the library.

- Restricted Access: Limited to a small group, offering a controlled sharing environment for photos and videos.

Shared Albums

- Sharing and Pooling: Create albums to share media with others.
- No Storage Impact: Shared Albums don't count against your or the recipients' iCloud storage quotas.
- Collaboration: Allow others to comment or add their own images and videos to the shared albums.
- Independent of iCloud Photos: You don't need to use iCloud Photos to utilize Shared Albums.

Understanding these distinctions can help you choose the right approach for managing and sharing your photos and videos across various devices and with different groups of people. Each feature comes with its own benefits and considerations, so selecting the most suitable option depends on your specific needs and preferences.

Syncing Your Photos Using iCloud

iCloud Photos offers a seamless way to sync your entire photo and video library across all your Apple devices, ensuring access to your media from anywhere. Here's an overview of how iCloud Photos manages storage and synchronization:

Full-Resolution Storage and Optimization

- Full-Resolution Storage: Apple stores original, full-resolution versions of your images and videos in the cloud, irrespective of the chosen optimization setting on your devices.
- Optimization Options: iOS/iPadOS and macOS provide an optimization option. When enabled, the device stores thumbnails instead of full-resolution copies, reducing local storage usage significantly.
- Space Management: Thumbnails take up minimal space, allowing for extensive library storage on the device without consuming excessive local storage.

Synchronization Process

- Thumbnail Retrieval: When media is added on other devices, only thumbnails are retrieved to the device with the optimization setting enabled.
- Cloud Uploads: Locally added media is uploaded to the cloud, and the full-resolution versions may be deleted from the device to free up space.
- On-Demand Retrieval: Full-resolution versions are fetched from iCloud when viewing, editing, or sharing media, ensuring optimal quality.

iCloud Storage Considerations

- Storage Tiers: iCloud storage tiers start at 50 GB, extending to 200 GB and 2 TB.
- 5 GB Limit: The free 5 GB storage included with iCloud is often insufficient, especially with extensive media usage. Upgrading to a higher iCloud+ tier is common for those with larger libraries or regular media capture.

By leveraging iCloud Photos and its optimization features, users can manage their photo and video libraries efficiently across devices while balancing local storage needs. However, due to the storage demands of extensive media usage, many users find upgrading to iCloud+ tiers necessary for a seamless experience.

Syncing iCloud Photos Across Your Devices

Enabling iCloud Photos across your devices ensures seamless synchronization of your media library. Here's how to set it up on various platforms:

Mac:

1. Open Photos App: Launch the Photos app on your Mac.

2. Access Settings: Navigate to Photos > Preferences > iCloud.

3. Enable iCloud Photos: Check the box for iCloud to activate iCloud Photos.

4. Choose Storage Option:

  - Download Originals to this Mac: Select this option if you have sufficient storage and want full-resolution local copies of all media.

  - Optimize Mac Storage: For limited local storage, allowing Photos to manage when to download or retain full-resolution versions automatically.

iOS/iPadOS:

1. Access Settings: Open Settings > Your Account Name > iCloud > Photos.

2. Enable iCloud Photos: Ensure "Sync this iPhone" or "Sync this iPad" is turned on under iCloud Photos.

3. Select Storage Option:

   - Download and Keep Originals: Keeps originals on the device if space allows.

   - Optimize Device Storage: Preserves thumbnails and manages storage by downloading full-resolution versions as needed.

Windows 11 (Using iCloud for Windows):

1. Open iCloud App: Launch the iCloud app on Windows 11.

2. Enable iCloud Photos: Ensure the Photos option is checked within the iCloud app.

3. Access Photo Options: Click "Options" next to Photos within the iCloud app.

4. Choose iCloud Photos: Select iCloud Photos to activate this feature.

Viewing iCloud Photos in Windows:

1. Using Microsoft Photos App: iCloud for Windows uses Microsoft Photos to display and manage iCloud Photos.

2. Access iCloud Photos: Open the Photos app and select iCloud Photos in the sidebar.

3. Ensure Visibility: If "iCloud Photos" isn't visible, access Settings within the Photos app and turn on "Show iCloud Photos."

By enabling iCloud Photos and choosing the appropriate storage option on each platform, you can effectively manage your media library across your devices while balancing local storage needs.

Learn More About iCloud Photos

Enabling iCloud Photos initiates a sync process between your devices and the iCloud storage. This synchronization uploads local media to iCloud and downloads any missing items from your iCloud library. While this setup offers seamless access to your media, there are several nuances and queries users often encounter:

1. Bandwidth Usage: iCloud Photos can consume substantial bandwidth during initial sync, but Apple has improved its efficiency over time.

  - Tip: Use the Pause button in the All Photos view of the Photos app to temporarily halt uploads/downloads.

2. Multiple Libraries on a Mac: While macOS allows multiple Photos libraries, only one can serve as the System Photo Library for iCloud Photos syncing. An exception exists for iCloud Shared Photo Libraries; this creates a second library synchronized via iCloud.

3. Handling Duplicates: iCloud Photos identifies identical media and stores a single copy while merging metadata.

4. Deletion Process: Deleting a photo moves it to the Recently Deleted album for about 30 days before permanent deletion. Recovery is possible within this period.

5. Library Contents and Uploads: Referenced images and non-imported media in the Mac Photos library might not be uploaded to iCloud Photos.

6. Merging Libraries: iCloud Photos syncs content between different Mac libraries when enabled on each device.

7. Turning Off iCloud Photos: Users are prompted to choose between keeping media locally or removing it when disabling iCloud Photos. Select accordingly to retain media.

8. Re-Enabling iCloud Photos: Upon reactivation, iCloud Photos verifies and syncs existing media rather than re-uploading or re-downloading everything.

Understanding these facets helps navigate iCloud Photos, offering insights into its functioning and assisting in troubleshooting potential issues.

Share Photos, Videos, and Albums

Shared Albums in iCloud Photos offer a convenient way to curate and share photos or videos with others. Here are some key aspects and limitations:

1. Shared Album Basics:

- Create and manage shared photo albums across various devices and platforms like macOS, iOS, iPadOS, iCloud.com, and Windows via the iCloud Shared Albums app.
- These albums can be publicly accessible as a website. You can also subscribe to albums shared by others.

2. Content Limits:

  - Albums are capped at 5,000 photos or videos each.

  - You can add up to 1,000 images per hour across all shared albums and up to 10,000 per day.

- A maximum of 200 shared albums can be created, and each album can have up to 100 subscribers.

3. Storage Considerations:

  - Media shared within these albums doesn't contribute to your iCloud storage usage.

  - Shared media remains accessible until the source media is deleted from your library or the shared album is removed.

4. Interactive Features:

  - Subscribers to shared albums can interact by commenting or liking photos.

  - If allowed, subscribers can also contribute their own photos and videos, subject to the 5,000-item limit.

5. Comment and Like Specifications:

  - Comments and captions associated with media can contain up to 200 characters.

  - New photos or comments on existing ones can be liked or commented on by subscribers.

6. Additional Details:

  - For comprehensive guidance on managing comments, likes, subscribers, and troubleshooting shared albums, refer to Apple's detailed support documentation.

Shared Albums are a versatile way to collaborate on visual content, offering a practical and user-friendly approach to collective photo or video sharing across multiple devices and users.

Enable Shared Albums

Enabling Shared Albums and sharing individual photos or videos is a great way to collaborate and distribute content across various devices. Here's a step-by-step guide to get started:

macOS:

1. Open Photos.
2. Navigate to Photos > Settings/Preferences > iCloud.
3. Select Shared Albums to enable this feature.

iOS/iPadOS:

1. Go to Settings.
2. Tap on your Account Name > iCloud > Photos.
3. Scroll to the bottom and toggle Shared Albums to enable it.

Windows:

1. Open the iCloud app.
2. Ensure that Photos is checked.
3. Click Options and select Shared Albums to enable this feature.

Share Photos or Videos Individually:

iOS/iPadOS:

1. Open the Photos or Camera app.

2. Navigate to the specific photos or videos you want to share.

3. Tap Select and choose the item(s) you wish to share.

4. Tap the Share icon.

5. Select Copy iCloud Link.

6. Paste the resulting URL into Messages, Mail, or any desired platform. Note that this link will expire after 30 days.

Sharing individual photos or videos allows you to distribute content seamlessly across various platforms while utilizing the convenience of iCloud's Shared Albums feature.

Share Photos from an iOS or iPadOS Device

Sharing photos and videos individually or within a shared album is a handy feature. Here are the steps to perform both actions on iOS or iPadOS:

Share Photos or Videos Individually:

1. Open the Photos or Camera app.

2. Navigate to the specific photos or videos you wish to share.

3. Tap Select and choose the item(s) you want to share.

4. Tap the Share icon.

5. Select Copy iCloud Link.

6. Paste the resulting URL into Messages, Mail, or any desired platform. Remember, this link will expire after 30 days.

Add Items to a Shared Album:

1. Open the Photos or Camera app.

2. Navigate to the specific photos or videos you want to add to a shared album.

3. Tap Select and choose the item(s) you want to share.

4. Tap the Share icon.

5. Select Add to Shared Album.

   - If you haven't created a shared album:

   - You'll be prompted to enter a name for a new album. Provide a name and tap Next. You can also create a new album by tapping Shared Album > New Shared Album, enter a name, and tap Next. Then, enter the name or email address of each contact you want to share the album with and tap Next.

   - If you've previously set up shared albums:

   - iCloud will default to the most recently used album. Enter an optional comment and tap Post to add items to this album.

   - To add items to a different existing album, tap Shared Album and select the desired album from the list.

6. Optionally, add a comment and tap Post.

These steps allow you to either individually share media via a link or add content to an existing or new shared album, facilitating easy collaboration and sharing among your contacts.

Sharing albums from Photos on a Mac is a simple process. Here's a step-by-step guide:

To Share an Album:

1. Select Images: Choose one or multiple images from any view in Photos.

2. Initiate Sharing:

   - Right-click (or Control-click) on the selected images.

   - Choose Share > Shared Albums from the contextual menu.

   - Alternatively, click the plus icon next to Shared Albums in the sidebar.

3. Share Dialog:

   - In the dialog box that appears:

     - Enter an optional comment for the shared album.

     - Click an existing shared album or select New Shared Album.

Creating a New Shared Album:

- If you choose New Shared Album:

  - Enter the album's name.

  - Add recipient(s) email addresses.

  - Optionally, include a comment.

  - Click Create.

Adjusting Settings and Web Access:

- To manage settings or enable web access for a shared photo album, follow these steps:

  - Select the shared album in the sidebar.

  - Click the People icon on the toolbar.

Importing Shared Photos to Your Library:

- While viewing a shared photo album, you can drag photos to your main Photos library to import them as you would with any other photo.

Deleting a Shared Album:

- To remove a shared photo album:

  - Right-click (or Control-click) the shared album name in the sidebar.

  - Choose Delete Shared Album from the contextual menu.

This process allows for efficient sharing of albums from your Mac's Photos app and provides options to customize settings and manage shared content effortlessly.

Share Albums from Windows

Sharing albums from Windows via the iCloud Shared Albums app is quite straightforward. Here's a step-by-step guide:

To Share Albums from Windows:

1. Launch iCloud Shared Albums:

   - Open the iCloud Shared Albums app on your Windows device.

2. Create a New Shared Album:

   - Click the "New shared album" button located in the upper-left corner of the app.

3. Set Up Album Details:

   - Enter the necessary album details:

     - Name the album in the Name field.

     - Optionally, check "Create a public website…" to generate an iCloud.com URL for sharing.

     - Add recipients by typing names or email addresses in the To field (matched from your contacts).

4. Proceed to Add Media:

   - Click Next.

   - Click "Choose photos or videos" to select media from your PC or iCloud Photos.

   - Navigate to the desired location and select the photos/videos you wish to add.

   - Click Open when you've made your selection.

5. Finish and Save:

   - Click Done to complete the process.

6. Access Album Settings:

   - To access album settings:

     - Right-click on an album in the main view.

- Choose "Stream options" from the menu.

   - Or, double-click an album and click Options.

7. Modify Album Settings:

   - In the settings, you can:

     - Change the album name.

     - Edit subscribers.

     - Toggle whether subscribers can add media to the album.

     - Enable/disable the album's visibility via a public website.

8. Access the Public Web View:

   - Right-click in the main album view or within the album's contents.

   - Choose "Open public web view" to access the album's URL on iCloud.com.

   - Copy the URL from the browser for sharing.

The iCloud Shared Albums app for Windows allows you to efficiently create, customize, and manage shared photo albums, providing various options for sharing with others.

Share a Photo Library

Setting up an iCloud Shared Photo Library offers a new way to share and collaborate on photos among a select group. Here's a concise guide to get started with this feature:

How to Set Up and Use iCloud Shared Photo Library:

1. Access Settings:

   - Open the Photos app on your macOS, iOS, or iPadOS device.

   - Navigate to Photos > Settings > Shared Library.

2. Initiate Setup:

   - Click on Get Started to initiate the setup process.

3. Follow Prompts:

   - Follow the on-screen prompts to set up your shared library.

   - You'll be given options to move all or specific photos, or delay moving any photos to the shared library.

4. Configure Settings:

   - After setup, revisit Photos > Settings > Shared Library to adjust various settings.

   - This is where you can manage settings related to your shared library, including preferences and criteria for sharing photos.

5. Access Shared Library:

   - Once set up, the shared library will be accessible within the Photos app on your macOS, iOS, or iPadOS devices.

   - You can also access it via the Photos web app on iCloud.com.

6. Work with Shared Photos:

- Participants in the shared library can add, delete, and edit photos, with changes visible to all participants.

- Shared photos will be available in Memories, Featured Photos, and the Photos widget for all participants.

7. Configure Display Options:

- Use the app's menu (on macOS, iOS, or iPadOS) to display your personal library, shared library, or both combined.

Setting up an iCloud Shared Photo Library allows for collaborative photo sharing and editing among a select group. It's a powerful feature for sharing memories and maintaining a collective album accessible to all participants. If you need more detailed instructions or settings, refer to Apple's guide or additional resources like Jason Snell's Take Control of Photos.

CHAPTER VIII: KEEP DOCUMENTS AND APP DATA IN SYNC

Enabling iCloud Drive allows you to synchronize your files and folders across multiple devices through the cloud. Here's how to get started and a preview of what to expect:

How to Enable iCloud Drive:

1. On macOS:

    - Open System Preferences.
    - Click on Apple ID and sign in if required.
    - Choose iCloud from the sidebar.
    - Ensure that iCloud Drive is checked.

2. On iOS/iPadOS:

    - Go to Settings.
    - Tap on your Apple ID at the top.
    - Select iCloud and toggle on iCloud Drive.

3. On Windows:

    - Install and open iCloud for Windows.
    - Check the box next to iCloud Drive.

4. Via iCloud Website:

- Access the iCloud website and sign in.
- Click on iCloud Drive.

Understanding iCloud Drive:

- Accessible Everywhere: iCloud Drive can be accessed through Finder (macOS), the Files app (iOS/iPadOS), Windows, iCloud website, and supported apps.
- Cloud-Based Storage: Your documents have an authoritative copy stored in the cloud. Your local devices also maintain copies.
- Synchronization: Changes made to iCloud Drive on one device sync across all others connected to the internet.

Exploring iCloud Drive:

- On a Mac or PC: Open Finder (Mac) or File Explorer (Windows) to access iCloud Drive. You'll find folders containing your files, and changes made will sync across devices.
- On iOS/iPadOS: Use the Files app to navigate iCloud Drive, where you can manage and organize your files similarly to Finder or File Explorer.

Understanding how iCloud Drive works and exploring its interface on different devices will help you effectively manage and synchronize your documents and files across your Apple ecosystem. Later, you can explore its functionality within various apps to leverage its syncing capabilities seamlessly.

Activate iCloud Drive

Activating iCloud Drive across your devices is crucial for seamless file synchronization. Here's how to activate and manage iCloud Drive settings:

Activation Steps:

1. On macOS:

    - Go to System Preferences > Apple ID > iCloud (Monterey or earlier) or System Settings > Account Name > iCloud (Ventura or later).

    - Enable iCloud Drive.

2. On iOS/iPadOS:

    - Navigate to Settings > Account Name > iCloud.

    - Toggle on iCloud Drive.

3. On Windows:

    - Open the iCloud app and check the iCloud Drive box.

Managing iCloud Drive Settings:

1. Prevent Apps from Using iCloud Drive:

    - Mac: Navigate to System Settings > Account Name > iCloud > iCloud Drive and click Options. Uncheck apps you don't want to use iCloud Drive. This hides the app's folder in iCloud Drive but doesn't affect data already saved or its appearance on other devices.

- iOS/iPadOS: Go to Settings > Account Name > iCloud > iCloud Drive. Turn off apps you want to disable on that device. Note that these apps lose in-app access to documents stored in iCloud Drive until reactivated, but you can still access their documents from the Files app.

2. Optimize Mac Storage (Mac Only):

- This setting manages local storage. It's detailed under Optimize Mac Storage.

3. Choose Apps for Email Look-Up:

- Mac: In System Settings > Account Name > iCloud > iCloud Drive, click Options > Look Me Up by Email to select apps for email look-up.
- iOS/iPadOS: Access Settings > Account Name > iCloud > Look Me Up.

These settings offer control over which apps use iCloud Drive, manage storage optimization, and control apps that use email look-up for sharing documents. Customizing these settings can enhance your iCloud Drive experience while ensuring security and efficient storage management.

Sync Your Desktop and Documents Folders (or Don't)

Enabling iCloud Drive to sync your Desktop and Documents folders across devices can be a convenient feature for many users. However, it's essential to understand the potential implications before diving in. Here's an overview:

How iCloud Syncs Desktop and Documents Folders:

Syncing Behavior: When activated, iCloud syncs the contents of your Desktop and Documents folders across all your Macs, iOS/iPadOS devices, and the iCloud website. Any changes or additions made to these folders on one device will reflect on others.

Convenience: It ensures seamless access to your crucial files across devices without the need for manual syncing, mirroring iCloud's handling of emails, contacts, calendars, and more.

Considerations Before Enabling Sync:

1. File Space: Large files or extensive data in these folders can consume significant iCloud storage. Ensure your iCloud storage plan accommodates your needs.
2. Internet Connection: Continuous syncing relies on a stable internet connection. Changes made offline will sync once online.
3. Privacy and Security: Uploaded files are stored on Apple's servers. Consider the sensitivity of the data you're syncing and ensure you're comfortable with it being stored on iCloud.

Activation:

On macOS:

- Navigate to System Preferences > Apple ID > iCloud.

- Check Desktop & Documents Folders.

Alternatives and Considerations:

- If you prefer not to use iCloud, other file-syncing services like Dropbox or Google Drive offer similar functionalities.

- Manually syncing files using external drives or third-party software is an alternative if you're concerned about using cloud-based services.

Understanding these aspects will help you make an informed decision about syncing your Desktop and Documents folders via iCloud Drive or seeking alternative methods that better align with your preferences and needs.

How Desktop & Documents Folder Syncing Works

When you opt to sync your Desktop and Documents folders using iCloud Drive, macOS initiates a relocation process. Here's what happens and what you should consider:

Folder Relocation:

1. Move to iCloud Drive: macOS shifts the Desktop and Documents folders from their original locations to the iCloud Drive folder.

2. Subfolders for Different Macs: The contents of each Mac's Desktop and Documents folders move to specific subfolders within iCloud Drive, named "Desktop - Mac Name" and "Documents - Mac Name."

Folder Syncing and iCloud Considerations:

1. Data Movement to iCloud: After relocation, these folders, like other iCloud Drive data, start syncing to Apple's servers and then to your other connected devices.

2. Storage Space: If your iCloud Drive lacks sufficient space for the added data, you'll be prompted to upgrade to a higher-tier iCloud+ plan.

3. Sync Time and Bandwidth: Uploading and downloading this data can take varying durations, from minutes to weeks, based on the volume of data and your internet speed.

Considerations for Large Files:

1. Syncing Challenges: Large files (such as gigabyte-sized files, virtual machines, or database software) can cause issues. Even minor changes prompt the entire file to resync across devices, consuming bandwidth and causing perpetual syncing.

2. Handling Large Files: It's advisable to relocate or manage such large files separately from the Desktop and Documents folders before activating syncing to avoid synchronization issues.

Syncing your Desktop and Documents folders with iCloud Drive offers convenience but comes with considerations regarding storage limits, sync duration, and challenges syncing large files. Managing larger files separately can help mitigate potential syncing problems for smoother operation.

Enabling iCloud Drive for Desktop & Documents folders comes with several important considerations:

1. Data Privacy Concerns: While iCloud Drive encrypts data in transit and on Apple's servers, this protection doesn't prevent Apple from accessing your data. In scenarios where demanded by government agencies, Apple is legally obliged and capable of providing access.

2. Optimize Mac Storage: If you enable Optimize Mac Storage alongside this feature, macOS may remove local copies of documents when your Mac runs low on disk space. This helps maintain file

access across multiple Macs but could lead to inconvenience if you lack internet access or have a slow connection when needing those files.

3. Folder Remapping: Enabling syncing relocates the Desktop and Documents folders to iCloud Drive. macOS transparently remaps these folders in the background, allowing applications and scripts referencing these locations to continue functioning normally.

4. Syncing Limitations: This feature syncs both Desktop and Documents folders; you can't selectively sync additional folders or choose to sync one without the other.

5. Disabling Syncing: If you turn off Desktop & Documents syncing, macOS won't restore data to its original locations automatically. It recreates empty folders at their original locations, leaving the iCloud Drive data untouched.

6. Suitability: This feature is most beneficial for users with multiple Macs, smaller Documents folder sizes, and less concern about data privacy. If these criteria don't align with your preferences or needs, leaving this option disabled might be a better choice.

If you find these considerations unsuitable for your needs, leaving this option disabled and exploring alternative methods might be more suitable for your workflow.

Enable Desktop & Documents Folder Syncing

To enable Desktop & Documents Folder Syncing:

1. Go to System Settings > Account Name > iCloud > iCloud Drive (Ventura or later) or System Preferences > Apple ID > iCloud (Monterey or earlier).

2. Click on the "Options" button next to iCloud Drive.

3. Check the "Desktop & Documents Folders" checkbox, then click "Done".

This change takes effect immediately, but the syncing process with Apple's servers may take some time to complete.

If you've used this feature on multiple Macs, by default, iCloud won't automatically merge these folders across your computers. Here's how you can manually merge these folders:

1. Open a Finder window and select iCloud Drive from the sidebar.
2. Inside iCloud Drive, locate one of the "Desktop - Mac Name" folders.
3. Drag the contents of that folder to your actual Desktop.
4. Repeat the process for each additional "Desktop - Mac Name" folder, but watch out for duplicates on your Desktop and manage them manually.
5. Delete all the empty "Desktop - Mac Name" folders from iCloud Drive.
6. Repeat the above steps for the Documents folders.

After performing these steps for both Desktop and Documents folders, your data should be successfully merged and synced across your Macs.

Disable Desktop & Documents Folder Syncing

To disable Desktop & Documents Folder Syncing:

1. Navigate to System Settings > Account Name > iCloud > iCloud Drive (Ventura or later) or System Preferences > Apple ID > iCloud (Monterey or earlier).
2. Click the "Options" button next to iCloud Drive.

3. Uncheck the "Desktop & Documents Folders" checkbox, then click "Turn Off" in the alert that appears, followed by "Done".

4. Click "OK" in the second alert confirming the change.

After disabling this feature, the items stored in iCloud Drive will remain there, and your local copies will vanish. If you wish to move them back to your Desktop and Documents folders:

1. Drag and drop the files back to their respective locations on your Desktop or in Documents.

2. Click "Move" in the alert confirming if you want to move the files out of iCloud Drive.

The download time to retrieve the files back to your Mac depends on the amount of data and your internet speed, especially if optimization was previously enabled.

If you choose to turn off iCloud Drive entirely while Desktop & Documents syncing is enabled or if you sign out of iCloud, iCloud will prompt you to choose what to do with your files:

- "Remove from Mac": Deletes the local copies. The originals remain on Apple's servers.
- "Keep a Copy": Creates an "iCloud Drive (Archive)" folder in your home directory, containing a copy of all iCloud Drive contents. You'll need to manually move these items to their intended locations. Originals stay on Apple's servers, and new Desktop and Documents folders are recreated in your home folder.

Alternative Methods for Syncing Desktop & Documents Without iCloud Drive

Using Resilio Sync Home, formerly known as BitTorrent Sync, offers an alternative method to sync your folders across devices without relying on iCloud Drive. This peer-to-peer technology connects your devices directly, using encrypted connections, eliminating the need for a central server.

Here's how it works and some benefits:

1. Syncing Across Devices: Resilio Sync allows syncing of folders across computers (Mac or PC) and NAS devices, accessible from iOS or iPadOS devices. However, access via web browsers isn't available as files aren't stored on a server.

2. File Size and Changes: The technology efficiently syncs changes almost instantly. For files over 4 MB that are modified, only the altered portions are transferred during sync, saving time and bandwidth.

3. Versions and Selective Sync: The Pro version ($59.90 for personal use) supports saving old and deleted file versions. It also offers Selective Sync, similar to iCloud Drive's Optimized Storage or Dropbox's Smart Sync. With Selective Sync, you can view folder contents on other devices without downloading the files until you explicitly request them or try to open them.

4. Pro Version Benefits: The Pro version is recommended for its ability to link all your devices, automatically syncing folders across them. Additionally, it provides Selective Sync functionality, which allows for greater control over which files sync to specific devices.

Considerations:

- The Pro version offers advanced features, making it suitable for personal use with a cost of $59.90. Family and business plans are also available.
- With Selective Sync enabled, you may not see thumbnails of graphics until they're downloaded to your computer.

Resilio Sync Home provides an efficient, peer-to-peer syncing solution across devices, ensuring data synchronization without relying on centralized servers.

Optimize Mac Storage

Enabling "Optimize Mac Storage" in iCloud Drive, accessible through System Settings or Preferences, allows your Mac to retain a local copy of all items in iCloud Drive, including your Desktop and Documents folders. However, if your disk space starts to diminish, older documents on your Mac are automatically deleted, leaving behind only their icons and metadata. When you access a deleted document, macOS fetches it from iCloud Drive, leading to a slightly longer opening time but otherwise transparent access.

This strategy mirrors the functionality of iCloud features like Music's Sync Library and iCloud Photos, adopting a similar approach for the broader iCloud documents.

While Optimize Mac Storage can be beneficial for users with limited local storage, it's not without risks. By activating this feature, you're trusting in the security of your data on Apple's servers, assuming there won't be any iCloud outages, relying on consistent internet connectivity for file retrieval, and entrusting macOS to make wise decisions about deleting older files from your Mac.

Ultimately, it's a personal choice whether to enable or disable this feature. Some may feel more secure keeping it disabled to have full control over their local files and avoid potential risks associated with relying on iCloud Drive for document storage and retrieval.

Exploring iCloud Drive on a Mac or PC is quite straightforward once it's activated:

On a Mac:

1. Finder Access: iCloud Drive is visible in the sidebar of the Finder. You can click on it or choose "Go > iCloud Drive" to access it directly.
2. Usage: Drag and drop files into or out of the iCloud Drive folder to move them to or from iCloud. Copying and pasting also work within this folder. You can organize items by creating folders or using standard file management methods.

On a PC (Windows):

1. File Explorer: iCloud Drive appears in the navigation pane of File Explorer just like any other folder.
2. Usage: Similar to the Mac, you can drag files into or out of the iCloud Drive folder in File Explorer, copy/paste files, create folders, and organize your items.

Accessing iCloud Drive on Unregistered Devices or for Collaboration:

- Web Access (iCloud Website): If you need access to your iCloud Drive from a device not signed in to your iCloud account or for real-time collaboration on iWork apps, you can use the iCloud website. It allows you to open documents from Pages, Numbers, and Keynote. For other files, you'll need compatible apps on the computer you're using.

When moving items out of iCloud Drive on a Mac or PC, you might encounter an alert asking for confirmation since removing items from this folder also deletes them from Apple's servers. It's essential to be cautious while managing files within iCloud Drive to avoid unintentional deletions.

Share Files and Folders on a Mac or PC

Sharing files and folders in iCloud Drive on a Mac or PC is an efficient way to collaborate or distribute content. Here's how you can do it:

Collaborate Mode:

1. Sharing Folders/Documents: Add files or folders to iCloud Drive, then right-click on the file/folder you want to share.

2. Select Share: Choose the "Share" option and then specify the people you want to invite to collaborate. You can set permissions for viewing, editing, and deleting items.

3. Invitations via Apple ID: People you invite need an Apple ID to access the shared items. If they don't have one, they'll be prompted to create an account for free.

Send Copy Mode:

1. Individual Sharing: For a static copy of a file or folder, you can send it via email, Messages, or other apps.

2. Access to Current Version: Recipients receive the current version of the file or folder but won't see any future changes you make.

Interface Changes:

- Ventura and Later: Apple revamped the interface and wording for sharing files and folders. In Ventura, you'll notice a more streamlined sharing interface and different terminology compared to older macOS versions like Monterey.

Collaborative Features:

- Edit Permissions: You can grant permission for recipients to make changes to the shared items or restrict them to view-only access.
- Link Sharing: Optionally, you can create a shareable link that allows access to the files or folders, even to those without an Apple ID.

Apple continuously updates its sharing features, so interface changes might be evident, but the core functionalities of collaborating and sharing files remain consistent across macOS versions.

In macOS Ventura or later, sharing files or folders from iCloud Drive involves a more streamlined process:

Share Items in macOS Ventura or Later:

1. Select File/Folder: Navigate to the file or folder you want to share within iCloud Drive using the Finder.
2. Click Share Icon: Once the file or folder is selected, click on the Share icon located in the toolbar. This action opens a popover menu (Figure 21).

Collaborate Mode:

If you choose Collaborate mode for sharing:

1. Adjust Sharing Options:

   a. Invited Access: Initially, the sharing defaults to allowing only invited people with edit permissions. Adjust settings by clicking "Only invited people can edit."

   b. Access Permissions: Select who can access the file/folder—either "Only invited people" or "Anyone with the link." Enable or disable the option to allow others to invite additional users.

   c. Editing Permissions: Set permissions for recipients—either "Can make changes" or "View only."

2. Distribution Methods:

   - Choose the sharing method: Mail, Messages, AirDrop, Invite with Link, or any supported app.

   - Enter the email addresses or phone numbers of the intended recipients if you chose "Only invited people."

   - Optionally, add a subject or message for context.

3. Share: Click on "Send," "Send Link," "Share Link," or an equivalent button. The wording might vary based on the selected app or method.

   - The link is sent through the selected method.

   - If using "Invite with Link," the link is copied to the Clipboard for manual distribution.

   - For Messages, the Messages app opens with a pre-filled share link; customize the message and recipients before sending.

This new sharing method streamlines the process by offering flexible permission settings and various distribution options right from the sharing popover.

For sharing files using the "Send Copy" mode:

Send Copy Mode:

1. Select Send Copy:

   - When opting for "Send Copy," the sharing options get more concise, displaying a narrowed-down list (Figure 22).

2. Choose Sharing Method:

   - Select a suitable sharing method from the available options, typically Mail, Messages, or AirDrop, based on your preference.

3. Add Details and Send:

   - Depending on the chosen method, include a subject or message as needed.

   - Proceed to send the file/folder via the selected method.

To modify sharing options later:

1. Access Shared Items:

   - Locate the shared item labeled as "Shared by Me" within iCloud Drive.

   - Right-click or Control-click on the item.

2. Manage Shared File/Folder:

   - Choose the option "Manage Shared File/Folder" from the context menu.

   - A dialog window opens, allowing you to:

- Add people to the shared item.

  - Remove individuals from the shared item.

  - Adjust permissions for specific users by hovering over their name and clicking the More icon.

  - Click "Stop Sharing" to cease sharing the item altogether.

This method enables you to revisit and modify sharing settings for the file or folder, providing control over access and permissions as needed.

For sharing items in macOS Monterey or earlier within iCloud Drive:

1. Select File or Folder:

  - Open Finder and choose a file or folder located inside iCloud Drive.

  - Click the Share icon on the toolbar.

2. Choose Share File or Share Folder:

  - A dialog box appears, presenting options to set access and permissions for sharing (Figure 23).

  - Configure the following settings:

    - "Who can access": Choose between "People you invite" or "Anyone with the link" to define the accessibility of the shared item.

    - Permission: Select "View only" or "Can make changes" to manage the level of access for those sharing the item.

- Tick the checkbox labeled "Anyone can add more people" to allow invited users to extend shared access.

3. Select Sharing Method:

   - Choose from options like Mail, Messages, Copy Link, AirDrop, or compatible third-party apps to distribute the shared item.

   - For Mail, AirDrop, and third-party apps, input email addresses or phone numbers for access.

   - For Messages and Copy Link, proceed to the next step.

4. Initiate Sharing:

   - Click "Share."

   - For Mail, AirDrop, and third-party apps, the link is sent via the selected method.

   - With Copy Link, the link is copied to the Clipboard for manual distribution.

   - With Messages, a Message dialog opens for customization before sending.

To modify sharing options afterward:

1. Access Shared Items:

   - Find the shared item labeled as "Shared by Me" in iCloud Drive.

   - Click the Share icon on the toolbar or right-click/Control-click on the item.

2. Manage Shared File/Folder:

   - Choose "Share" > "Manage Shared File/Folder" from the context menu.

- A dialog box opens, enabling actions like adding or removing people, adjusting individual permissions, or stopping sharing entirely.

Share Items on a PC

To share iCloud Drive files and folders on a PC:

1. Initiate Sharing:

   - Right-click on a file or folder within iCloud Drive.

   - Choose "Share with iCloud Drive" > "Share File" or "Share Folder" from the context menu.

2. Set Initial Sharing Options:

   - In the dialog box that appears, configure the following initial sharing settings:

     - "Who can access": Select between "Only people you invite" or "Anyone with the link" to define access permissions.

     - Permission: Choose "View only" or "Can make changes" to control the level of access for shared users.

     - Check the box labeled "Anyone can add more people" to allow invited users to extend shared access.

     - For invited users, input their email addresses or phone numbers. Modify individual permissions by clicking the More icon next to each person's name in the list.

3. Start Sharing:

   - Click "Apply" to initiate sharing. A "Share link" dialog box opens.

- Use the provided options to email listed contacts or click "Copy link" to copy the link to your clipboard. Share the link via email, instant messaging, or any preferred method.

To modify sharing options later:

1. Access Sharing Settings:

   - Right-click the shared item again within iCloud Drive.

   - Choose "Share with iCloud Drive" > "Manage Shared File or Folder" from the context menu.

2. Manage Sharing:

   - The same dialog box reappears, allowing you to:

     - Add or remove people.

     - Modify individual permissions.

     - Click "Stop Sharing" to terminate sharing for the item.

Use iCloud Drive Within Mac Apps

Using iCloud Drive within Mac apps can vary based on app-specific integration:

1. Open and Save Dialogs: Most apps feature iCloud Drive in the sidebar of their Open and Save dialogs. This allows manual navigation within iCloud Drive to access or store documents. If you don't see the sidebar in a Save dialog, click the disclosure button next to the filename field or select "Other" from the Where menu to expand the dialog.

2. Explicit iCloud Drive Support: Certain apps explicitly designed for iCloud Drive may display an extra entry in the sidebar, labeled with the app's name, under iCloud in Open and Save dialogs. This serves as a shortcut to the app's specific iCloud Drive folder.

3. App-Specific Folder Visibility: Developers have the option to hide their app's folder on specific platforms. Consequently, the sidebar entry within the app may be the only way to access that app's documents. These folders might not be visible in the Finder or on the iCloud website.

4. File Type Restrictions: Developers can also define which file types their app-specific folder supports. For instance, an app may not allow certain file formats to be stored in its folder. If an app can't open a particular file format, it may restrict users from placing that file type in its designated iCloud Drive folder.

App-specific iCloud Drive folders offer a convenient way to interact with an app's documents. However, the visibility and functionality of these folders can vary depending on how developers choose to implement iCloud Drive integration within their applications.

Use the Files App for iOS or iPadOS

The Files app in iOS and iPadOS provides access to iCloud Drive and various other apps and cloud services. Here's how to navigate iCloud Drive within the Files app:

On iPhone or iPod Touch:

1. Open the Files app.

2. You might see recently added or modified files at the top and a list of locations at the bottom. Tap "Recents" or "Browse" to switch between these views.

3. If you're in the Browse view and see a list of locations, tap "iCloud Drive" to access its contents.

4. If you're already in another location, tap the label in the upper-left corner of the screen to move up a level. Repeat until you find the "Locations" list, then tap "iCloud Drive."

On iPad:

1. Open the Files app.

2. The iPad typically displays a sidebar with categories like Recents and Locations. If you don't see it, tap the Sidebar icon at the top to reveal it.

3. In the sidebar, tap "iCloud Drive" to explore its contents.

Additional Features:

- iPhone: Tap the More icon (three dots) to reveal additional commands like "New Folder," switch between Icons and List view, and adjust the sort order.

- iPad: Tap the View icon (grid, list, or columns) to access different view options like Icons, List, and Columns. You can also tap the New Folder icon to create a new folder.

These options allow you to manage your iCloud Drive files, create folders, change views, and organize your documents directly within the Files app on your iOS device.

That's a comprehensive set of actions you can take within the Files app for iCloud Drive:

1. Open: Tap a file to open it with its default app.

2. Rename: Touch and hold the file, then tap Rename from the popover. Note that renaming certain folders, especially those tied to specific apps, might not be possible.

3. Delete: Tap Select, choose the file, and then tap the Trash icon or the word Delete to remove it.

4. Move: Tap Select, select the file, tap the Folder icon or the word Move, navigate to a new location, and tap Move. However, not all locations may be viable destinations.

5. Share: Tap Select, choose the file/folder, tap the Share icon, and select Send Copy or Collaborate. For Collaborate, further sharing options are available, similar to those in macOS Ventura or later.

6. Zip/Unzip: Tap Select, select the file, tap More or the More icon, and then choose Compress or Uncompress.

7. Search: Utilize the Search field at the top to search for files across your entire iCloud Drive.

These functionalities empower users to manage and interact with their files and folders conveniently within the Files app on iOS and iPadOS.

Absolutely, the Files app serves as a centralized hub to access various cloud-connected services and locations, making file management more streamlined across different platforms. Here's a rundown of how you can access and manage files from different sources within the Files app:

1. Supported Services: iCloud Drive, Dropbox, Google Drive, OneDrive, Transmit, Resilio Sync, DEVONthink To Go, local Macs with file sharing enabled, and files stored locally on your iOS/iPadOS device in the "On My Device" category.

2. Navigation: Start by tapping "Locations" on the Browse screen, allowing you to navigate to different connected services. The interface for each service will vary, reflecting the design and features of the respective service or app.

3. Adding/Disabling Locations: You can manage these locations by tapping the More icon, then selecting Edit or Edit Sidebar. From here, you can toggle switches to enable or disable specific locations. Additionally, you can rearrange their order by dragging the handle icon.

4. Interface Variance: Each location or service within the Files app will have its unique interface and features, similar to their respective stand-alone apps. Despite slight differences, they maintain enough similarity for intuitive navigation.

The Files app's unified approach facilitates easy access and management of files across different cloud services and local devices, making it a versatile tool for users dealing with various file sources and types.

Use iCloud Drive Within iOS and iPadOS Apps

Accessing iCloud Drive within iOS and iPadOS apps varies in terms of accessibility and visibility. Here are some general guidelines and specific examples for navigating iCloud Drive within various apps:

1. Document Picker Interface: Most apps that support iCloud Drive will incorporate a document picker interface resembling the Files app. However, some apps might primarily display only their own documents, making it necessary to explore further to find iCloud Drive.
2. Default Views: Some apps, like Pages, Numbers, and Keynote, might default to displaying recent documents. To access iCloud Drive, tap on "Browse" or navigate to the upper-left corner to switch to iCloud Drive's top-level view.
3. Specific App Instructions:
    - Pages, Numbers, and Keynote: Initially might display recent documents; to access iCloud Drive, tap on "Browse" or navigate from the upper-left corner.
    - GoodReader: Tap on "Manage Files," then "Import Files," followed by "Open from Files" or "Import from Files."

- Documents by Readdle: Navigate through "My Files" > "Files" > "Browse" to reach the top level of iCloud Drive.

4. App Specifics: Some apps might not fully support iCloud Drive or could have the document picker located in an unexpected place. In such cases, reaching out to the developer for guidance might be helpful.

While most apps provide access to iCloud Drive and the document picker, the location and visibility of this feature can vary. Exploring different areas within the app or checking for specific guidance from the app's developer can help locate iCloud Drive for seamless file access and management.

Troubleshoot iCloud Drive

Troubleshooting iCloud Drive syncing issues can be a bit intricate, but here are some steps to resolve common problems:

1. Ensure Account Sign-In: Verify that you are signed in with the same Apple ID across all your devices in System Settings (on Mac) or System Preferences > Apple ID. Consistency in the signed-in account is crucial for iCloud Drive syncing.

2. Restarting Background Processes: In Terminal, you can restart the background processes related to iCloud Drive by entering the following command:

```
killall bird; killall cloudd
```

Press Return after entering the command. This action usually nudges iCloud Drive syncing back into operation.

3. All-Purpose iCloud Troubleshooting: Follow the comprehensive iCloud troubleshooting procedure you previously mentioned, which involves checking Apple's status page and attempting to resolve issues systematically.

4. Using Cirrus App: Consider using the Cirrus app for accessing logs and status information on iCloud processes. However, note that interpreting these logs requires technical expertise.

5. Apple Support Articles: Apple provides helpful resources through its iCloud Drive FAQ and a guide on setting up iCloud Drive on an iPhone. These articles might contain specific solutions or guidance for common issues.

These steps cover a range of potential problems and troubleshooting methods. Remember, iCloud Drive issues can sometimes be complex, so seeking help from Apple's support resources or community forums can also be beneficial.

Use In-App Data Syncing

In-app data syncing via iCloud has become an integral part of many applications, allowing seamless synchronization across multiple devices. Here are some examples and considerations regarding this functionality:

1. BBEdit: This text editor synchronizes settings, scripts, plugins, and other data via iCloud across different Macs, ensuring a consistent experience on each device.

2. Hazel: This utility, used for automated actions on specified folders, utilizes iCloud for syncing rules across Macs, enabling uniform automation setups on different machines.

3. Apple's Podcasts App: iCloud syncing in Podcasts manages custom stations and playback positions, enabling a seamless transition from one device to another while listening to podcasts.

Besides these specific apps, iCloud Drive synchronizes various other data and settings across devices:

- Text abbreviations

- Apple Mail settings: Signatures, flag names, blocked senders, muted conversations, rules, and smart mailboxes

However, it's essential to note that not all apps support iCloud syncing by default. Developers must explicitly integrate iCloud syncing into their apps. While some apps, like Apple's Podcasts, have iCloud syncing automatically enabled without a user-disable option, third-party apps often require manual activation of this feature.

Checking an app's preferences or settings is the usual way to determine if iCloud syncing is supported and how to enable it. Typically, enabling iCloud syncing in third-party apps involves toggling a switch or selecting iCloud from a dropdown menu within the app settings.

Lastly, it's important to recognize that iCloud syncing is limited to Macs and iOS/iPadOS devices. If you're using an app available across different operating systems like Windows, Linux, or Android, alternative syncing methods such as Dropbox might be more suitable for cross-platform data synchronization.

About Optimized Storage

Optimized Storage is Apple's umbrella term for a range of features aimed at efficiently managing disk space on your Mac. While the specific components included might not be explicitly listed by Apple, several functionalities are typically associated with Optimized Storage:

1. Automatic Cleanup: macOS automatically clears certain caches, logs, and redundant downloads to free up space. Users generally have limited control over these automated processes.

2. Storage Management in System Information: The Storage Management tool in System Information displays the storage used by different apps and files, allowing users to delete unnecessary items that might be consuming space.

3. Automatic Trash Emptying: There's an option to have macOS automatically empty the Trash after 30 days, reducing the clutter of deleted files.

4. Media Management in Music/iTunes: Users can choose to automatically delete purchased movies and TV shows after watching them, giving the option to re-download them later if necessary.

5. Apple Mail Attachment Preferences: Users can specify whether Apple Mail should download all, none, or only recent email attachments, managing the amount of local storage used by mail attachments.

6. iCloud Photos Optimization: In Photos, the "Optimize Mac Storage" setting replaces full-resolution local copies of photos with smaller versions if disk space becomes limited (covered in the Sync with iCloud Photos feature).

7. Storage of Desktop and Documents Folders in iCloud Drive: iCloud Drive can store Desktop and Documents folders, allowing access and synchronization across devices (covered in the Sync Your Desktop and Documents Folders feature).

8. Optimize Mac Storage for iCloud Drive: Similar to iCloud Photos, this setting optimizes storage by storing less frequently accessed files in iCloud, freeing up local space.

It's noteworthy that only the last three features listed directly involve iCloud and are discussed in this book, as iCloud-related functionalities are the focus here. These features leverage iCloud's capabilities to manage and optimize storage across Apple devices.

CHAPTER IX: KEEP MAIL, CONTACTS, AND CALENDARS IN SYNC

Syncing email, contacts, and calendars across your Apple devices is crucial for seamless coordination. While these functions use distinct technologies, they all synchronize through iCloud. When you modify email content, contacts, or calendar entries on one device, iCloud promptly updates these changes across your other connected devices.

This chapter will delve into these three data types. To keep things straightforward, I've skipped the mundane instructions for tasks you likely understand or can explore easily on your own. Apple often provides detailed guidance via the Help menu on your Mac or through their iCloud User Guide, which covers various aspects of managing these functions.

Work with iCloud Mail

Indeed, an iCloud account comes with an email address using the icloud.com domain and offers a minimum storage space of 5 GB, which is shared among various iCloud services. The web interface for iCloud Mail provides a convenient way to access your emails (refer to The Mail Web App for more details).

Primarily, iCloud Mail functions as a typical IMAP (Internet Message Access Protocol) account. This means that your email messages, including those in your inbox, sorted folders, and sent items, are stored on your email host's mail server. Additionally, the server keeps track of various actions such as reading, replying to, or forwarding messages. Because the emails are stored remotely, you can access them from any device, including third-party email clients or web browsers. This consistency ensures that you see the same emails in the same locations with the same statuses across all devices. Notably, iCloud Mail does not support POP (Post Office Protocol) at all.

iCloud Mail operates on IMAP principles, allowing seamless synchronization of emails across devices without manual intervention, thanks to the inherent nature of IMAP. However, iCloud Mail offers a few distinctive features that set it apart from typical IMAP accounts:

1. Ease of Setup: Enabling iCloud Mail on any Apple device is incredibly straightforward. After entering your iCloud username and password, simply turning on the Mail option is all that's required to set it up.

2. Push Updates: When used on iOS and iPadOS devices, iCloud Mail offers push updates. This means messages are instantly delivered to your device as soon as they arrive, instead of waiting for scheduled checks.

3. Webmail Interface: iCloud Mail provides a robust webmail interface. This interface supports various functionalities such as searching message contents, setting up auto-responses, forwarding emails, utilizing Mail Drop for attachments, and creating rules to automatically manage messages.

4. Spam and Malware Filtering: Apple's mail servers include basic spam and malware filtering. However, iCloud Mail might silently delete certain incoming messages without notifying the sender or recipient if the message matches undisclosed criteria, as explained in an article on Macworld. This approach may result in the deletion of potentially legitimate emails, which can be a concern.

5. Aliases: iCloud Mail allows the addition of up to three aliases, which are additional email addresses using the @icloud.com domain. These aliases forward incoming messages to your primary inbox. You can create rules specifically for these aliases, similar to your primary email address, enabling separate processing or forwarding of these messages.

6. Hide My Email: This feature allows you to create an anonymous alias managed by Apple directly within a message you're composing, providing additional privacy.

7. Custom Domain Support: iCloud Mail, with an iCloud+ subscription, enables the use of a custom domain name. This feature allows the use of up to three addresses within that custom domain, similar to iCloud aliases.

8. Syncing Settings: While enabling Mail in iCloud syncs messages and mailboxes across devices, additional Mail settings and data such as signatures, flag names, blocked senders, muted conversations, rules, smart mailboxes (on Macs), VIPs, and previous recipients sync only when iCloud Drive is enabled, and Mail is selected in iCloud Drive options.

Overall, iCloud Mail is a decent email service but might not offer the same level of customization or extensive features compared to other email providers. Users looking for more extensive options or specific features might find services like Gmail, Outlook.com, Yahoo, or various other providers more suitable. These alternatives may offer more services, security options, or increased storage, making them viable choices for primary or secondary email accounts. Users have the freedom to opt-out of iCloud Mail or use it as a secondary account if its limitations are not preferable.

iCloud Mail offers some distinctive features that set it apart from standard IMAP accounts:

1. Ease of Setup: Setting up an iCloud Mail account on Apple devices is incredibly straightforward—just enable Mail after entering your iCloud credentials.

2. Push Updates: iOS and iPadOS devices allow users to opt for push updates, ensuring immediate message delivery rather than waiting for scheduled checks.

3. Webmail Interface: iCloud Mail offers a user-friendly web interface with powerful features like search within message content, auto-responses, forwarding options, Mail Drop for attachments, and customizable message sorting rules.

4. Mail Filtering: While Apple's servers provide basic spam and malware filtering, it's noted that iCloud Mail sometimes summarily deletes incoming messages that meet certain criteria without notifying the sender or recipient. This approach contrasts with typical spam handling methods that move messages to a designated Junk or Spam mailbox.

5. Email Aliases: Users can create up to three @icloud.com email aliases that redirect incoming messages to the primary Inbox, allowing distinct handling through customized rules.

Regarding accessing iCloud Mail using other email clients, setting up an alternate email client to access iCloud Mail is possible. Here are the IMAP settings:

- Incoming Mail (IMAP) server: imap.mail.me.com
- Username: Your full Apple ID
- Password: An app-specific password (see Use App-Specific Passwords)
- IMAP authentication method: Use "password"
- SSL for incoming mail: Yes
- Port: 993

- Outgoing (SMTP) mail server: smtp.mail.me.com
- SMTP Authentication: Yes; use "password"
- SSL for outgoing mail: Yes
- SMTP port: 587

These settings should enable the configuration of iCloud Mail on various email clients across different platforms, including Windows and Linux.

Use Mail Drop

Mail Drop is a nifty feature within iCloud that simplifies sending large attachments via email, particularly when dealing with file size limitations. Here's how it works across different platforms:

Activation:

- iOS and iPadOS: Mail Drop is automatically enabled and available within the Mail app.
- macOS: For iCloud email accounts, Mail Drop is typically enabled by default. For other accounts (IMAP or Exchange), access Mail > Preferences > Accounts > Account Name > Account Information, and select "Send large attachments with Mail Drop" to activate it.
- iCloud Web App: Access the Mail web app on the iCloud website, click the gear icon, choose Preferences, click Composing, and check "Use Mail Drop when sending large attachments" to enable it.

How It Works:

1. Compose Email: Start composing an email and attach files as usual.

2. Sending Process: When the combined size of the email and its attachments exceeds a certain limit (around 20 MB), Mail recognizes this and triggers Mail Drop.

3. Attachment Handling: Instead of sending the files directly, Mail uploads the attachments to iCloud and inserts a link to the files within the email.

4. Recipient Experience: The recipient receives the email with a link to download the attachments from iCloud. Mail Drop attachments do not consume the recipient's mailbox space.

5. Storage Duration: Attachments sent via Mail Drop are stored on iCloud for 30 days before automatic deletion, ensuring space efficiency.

This feature eliminates the hassle of dealing with file size restrictions when sending attachments and provides a smooth and streamlined process for both the sender and recipient.

Sync Your Contacts

iCloud Contacts is a powerful tool that keeps your address book consistent across all your devices. Here are a couple of notable aspects of iCloud Contacts:

Seamless Syncing:

- Instant Sync: iCloud Contacts immediately updates any changes or additions across all your connected devices.

- Merge Contacts: Enabling Contacts sync might prompt you to merge existing local contacts with those on iCloud. It's usually recommended to merge them.

- Turning Off Sync: Disabling iCloud Contacts may ask if you want to delete local contacts. In most cases, it's advisable to retain these contacts locally.

Quirks to Note:

Two particular elements of iCloud Contacts might seem unconventional or slightly problematic:

1. Duplicate Contacts: Occasionally, duplicate contacts may appear due to various reasons like multiple sync sources. Cleaning up duplicates manually or using built-in cleanup tools could be necessary.

2. Contact Versioning: iCloud sometimes saves multiple versions of the same contact, especially after changes. This versioning can lead to confusion if not managed properly.

Troubleshooting any discrepancies or issues with your contacts could involve merging duplicates, managing versioning, or addressing syncing conflicts. If you encounter problems, the Troubleshoot Contact and Calendar Problems section might offer valuable assistance.

Understanding these quirks can help you effectively manage your contacts on iCloud and ensure a streamlined experience across your devices.

Work with Contact Groups

Working with contact groups in iCloud can streamline communication. Here's what you need to know:

Creating and Utilizing Groups:

- Group Creation: Use the Contacts app on iCloud's website or macOS to create groups, like a sports team or work department.

- Sending Messages: Once groups are created, you can easily address emails to the entire group by typing its name in the To, Cc, or Bcc field in Mail.

iOS and iPadOS Limitations:

- iOS/iPadOS Versions: In older versions (before iOS/iPadOS 16), creating groups directly in Contacts was unavailable. Removing members from groups had to be done on macOS or the Contacts web app.

- Smart Groups Absence: Smart groups created on macOS don't appear in Contacts on iOS/iPadOS. This absence affects Mail functionality on these devices.

Groups are mainly used for efficient communication, allowing you to easily message an entire group of contacts without having to select individual recipients each time. However, the limitations in iOS and iPadOS versions might affect group management, requiring actions to be performed on a Mac or iCloud's web interface.

Understanding these limitations helps manage expectations when working with contact groups across different Apple devices.

Share Your Contacts with Someone Else

Sharing contacts through iCloud isn't directly supported as it is with calendars. However, there are workarounds if you want to collaborate on contacts with family members or others:

Workaround Solution:

1. Secondary iCloud Account: Create a secondary iCloud account specifically for shared contacts.

2. Limited Services: On each device involved, add this shared account and enable only the Contacts service, disabling other services to prevent clutter.

3. Move Contacts: Transfer the contacts you want to share to this shared account, removing them from individual accounts to avoid confusion.

Variations:

- Single Shared iCloud Account: Instead of creating a new shared account, one person can add their iCloud account as secondary on others' devices, ensuring only Contacts are enabled.

- Default Account Check: Ensure the default contacts account on each iOS/iPadOS device is set correctly to avoid new contacts ending up in the wrong place.

Downsides and Caveats:

- "Me" Card Conflict: Using multiple iCloud accounts might lead to conflicts with the "me" card, causing shared "me" cards across devices, affecting personalization.

Remember, these workarounds aren't official solutions and might have limitations or unintended consequences, like the "me" card issue. It's a way to share contacts, but it's not as seamless or supported as other iCloud features like calendar sharing.

Sync Your Calendars

Calendars on iCloud work seamlessly across your devices, updating events automatically and offering a range of useful features. However, managing meeting invitations and shared calendars might require a bit more attention. Let me elaborate on these aspects:

Handling Meeting Invitations:

- Accept/Decline Invitations: When receiving a meeting invitation via Calendar, you can accept or decline it. iCloud syncs these responses across your devices.

- Update Meetings: Accepted invitations sync changes made to meeting details, ensuring everyone involved stays informed.

- Invitations via Email: In some cases, meeting invitations might come via email; accepting them directly from the email should also update your iCloud Calendar.

Managing Shared Calendars:

- Sharing Calendars: iCloud allows you to share specific calendars with other iCloud users. This feature is useful for family events, work schedules, or group planning.

- Invite Others: You can invite people to view or edit shared calendars, keeping everyone in sync with the latest updates.

- Access from Web: iCloud's web interface allows access to shared calendars, enabling users without Apple devices to view or contribute to shared events.

Troubleshooting Calendar Issues:

- Troubleshoot Problems: If you encounter issues with calendar syncing or invitations not updating, refer to troubleshooting tips in Calendar settings or iCloud support documentation.

- Sync and Refresh: Sometimes manually refreshing or syncing the calendar on devices might resolve discrepancies or delays in updates.

Understanding these aspects can streamline your experience with iCloud Calendar, particularly when collaborating with others or managing event invitations. If you encounter any issues, exploring troubleshooting options or referring to support resources can be helpful.

CHAPTER X: SYNC OTHER ICLOUD DATA

Absolutely, iCloud seamlessly synchronizes a wide range of data beyond the commonly highlighted features like email, contacts, and calendars. Here's a rundown of some of the less talked about but equally crucial data iCloud synchronizes:

Safari Bookmarks, iCloud Tabs, and Reading List:

- Safari Sync: iCloud keeps your bookmarks synced across devices, enabling you to access your favorite websites from any Apple device.

- iCloud Tabs: You can see tabs open on one device across all other iCloud-linked devices.

- Reading List: Save articles or webpages to your Reading List on one device and access them later from any iCloud-linked device.

Health App Data:

- Health Data Sync: Data tracked by the Health app, such as fitness stats, vital signs, or health-related information, syncs across devices for a comprehensive view of your health metrics.

Siri Data:

- Siri Sync: iCloud syncs some Siri-related data, such as your Siri settings and preferences, enhancing your voice assistant experience across devices.

Reminders, Notes, and Messages:

- Reminders and Notes: iCloud ensures your Reminders and Notes are updated across devices in real-time, allowing seamless access and management.

- iMessage Conversations: Messages sync across Apple devices, enabling you to continue conversations from any device.

Other Built-in Apple Apps:

- News, Stocks, Home, Voice Memos: Data and preferences from these apps also sync via iCloud, maintaining consistency across your Apple ecosystem.

While these functionalities might not grab headlines, they play a significant role in providing a cohesive and unified experience across your Apple devices. The behind-the-scenes synchronization ensures that your data and preferences are available wherever and whenever you need them.

Sync Messages

Absolutely, enabling Messages in iCloud is a great way to keep your iMessage and SMS conversations synchronized across all your Apple devices. Here's how you can enable Messages in iCloud on your Mac and iOS/iPadOS devices:

On a Mac:

1. Open the Messages app.

2. Navigate to Messages > Preferences > iMessage > Settings.

3. Check the box next to "Enable Messages in iCloud."

4. You can force an immediate sync by clicking on "Sync Now."

On iOS/iPadOS:

1. Open the Settings app.

2. Tap on your Apple ID at the top.

3. Select "iCloud" (or "Show All" and then "Messages" in iOS 15/iPadOS 15).

4. Toggle on "Sync this iPhone" or "Sync this iPad" (iOS 16/iPadOS 16 or later) or simply enable the "Messages" option (iOS 15/iPadOS 15).

After enabling Messages in iCloud on all your devices, your messages will start syncing automatically. The time taken for the initial sync depends on the volume of message data and your internet connection speed.

This feature not only synchronizes your messages across devices but also utilizes optimized storage by storing older messages and their attachments in iCloud, helping to free up space on your devices while keeping your conversation history intact.

Use Location-Based Reminders

Setting up location-based reminders is a great way to prompt yourself with tasks based on your geographic location. Here's how you can do it across your Apple devices:

On Mac:

1. Open the Reminders app and select the reminder you want to associate with a location.

2. Click on the "Info" icon.

3. Choose "At a Location."

4. Enter the address, select a contact's address, or choose "Current Location."

5. Pick "Arriving" or "Leaving" for the alert.

6. Click "Done."

On iOS/iPadOS:

1. Open the Reminders app and select the reminder.

2. Tap the "Info" icon.

3. Choose "Remind Me at a Location."

4. Enter the address, choose a contact's address, or pick "Current Location."

5. Select "Arriving" or "Leaving" for the alert.

6. Tap "Done."

Once set up, when you approach or leave the designated location, your device should notify you with the reminder. Just remember that external factors like network connectivity can occasionally impact the precision of these location-based alerts.

Work with Notes

The Notes app is packed with features that make it a versatile tool for storing various kinds of information across your Apple devices. Here's a rundown of the capabilities available in the Notes app:

- Text Formatting: Create plain or styled text with headings, lists (bulleted, dashed, numbered), checklists, tables, limited paragraph styles, and text attributes like bold, italic, or underline.

- Attachments: Attach files such as photos, videos, sounds, and PDFs to your notes. You can also include URLs and even scan documents directly within the app.

- Drawing and Sketching: Sketch with your finger or a stylus, insert sketches into your notes, and use the camera to "scan" documents. You can also intersperse sketches with typed text.

- Share and Collaboration: Share content from various apps directly to Notes, and collaborate with others by allowing them to edit shared notes.

- Voice Memos Integration: Record voice memos using the Voice Memos app and share them directly to your Notes.

- Password Protection: Lock individual notes with a password for added security. Keep in mind that forgetting the password can result in permanently locked notes.

- Instant Notes: Quickly start a note by tapping your iPad's Lock screen with an Apple Pencil or by using the Notes button in Control Center (customizable in Settings).

These features make Notes a versatile tool for storing different types of information and collaborating with others efficiently across your Apple devices.

Sync Data from Other Apps

iCloud offers the option to sync data from various native Apple apps across your devices. Here's a breakdown of how you can enable syncing for these apps:

- Health: If you want to sync health-related data from the Health app on your iPhone to other iPhones or devices, you can enable this through iCloud settings. Simply navigate to Settings > [Your Name] > iCloud on your iPhone and toggle on Health.

- Siri: Siri's learning and customization can be synced across your Macs, iPhones, and iPads using iCloud. To activate this feature on a Mac, go to System Preferences > [Your Apple ID] > iCloud (Ventura or later) or System Preferences > Apple ID > iCloud (Monterey or earlier) and enable Siri. On an iOS or iPadOS device, navigate to Settings > [Your Name] > iCloud and turn on Siri.

- Other Built-in Apps: Several other Apple apps like Freeform, Game Center, Home, News, Stocks, Voice Memos, and Wallet offer data syncing through iCloud. You can manage their syncing preferences individually. These apps typically have their checkboxes or switches in the iCloud settings. For instance, Voice Memos syncing can be enabled or disabled by going to iCloud settings, clicking on Options for iCloud Drive, and toggling the Voice Memos option.

Enabling these options ensures that data from these apps stays in sync across your Apple devices, providing a seamless experience and access to your information wherever you go.

Use Universal Clipboard

Universal Clipboard is indeed a fantastic feature that simplifies the copy-paste process between your Apple devices. To ensure it works seamlessly, here are the key requirements and settings needed:

1. Device Compatibility: Make sure your devices meet the compatibility criteria. For Macs, the model should be from 2012 or later (2013 or later for Mac Pro). iOS devices should be running iOS 10 or later, and iPadOS devices should be running iPadOS 13 or later.

2. Operating System Versions: Ensure all devices are running macOS Sierra 10.12 or later, iOS 10 or later, or iPadOS 13 or later.

3. Wi-Fi Connection: All devices should be connected to the same Wi-Fi network.

4. Bluetooth Enabled: Bluetooth needs to be activated on all devices and within range of each other (usually within the same room) for Universal Clipboard to function properly.

5. iCloud Account: All devices should be signed in to the same primary iCloud account. This ensures that the clipboard data can be synced across devices seamlessly.

6. Handoff Enabled: Handoff needs to be turned on across your devices. In macOS Ventura or later, navigate to System Preferences > AirDrop & Handoff. In macOS Monterey or earlier, go to System Preferences > General. On iOS/iPadOS devices, you can find Handoff settings under Settings > General > AirPlay & Handoff.

Once these conditions are met, Universal Clipboard should work smoothly, allowing you to copy content on one device and paste it directly into an app on another device, simplifying your workflow between Apple devices.

CHAPTER XI: WORK WITH ICLOUD KEYCHAIN

iCloud Keychain serves as a convenient and secure method to manage and sync sensitive data like passwords, credit card information, and more across your Apple devices. Here are some of its key features and functionalities:

1. Syncing Passwords and Data: iCloud Keychain syncs your passwords, credit card details (excluding the CVV number), and other crucial data across all your Apple devices. This allows Safari to autofill credentials on any device you're using, regardless of where you initially entered the information.

2. Managing Credit Card Information: It provides a secure platform to store credit card information for autofill in web forms, excluding the CVV number.

3. Multiple Credential Sets: You can create multiple sets of login credentials for a single site or credentials that work across different subdomains of the same site.

4. One-Time Codes for 2FA: Enables the use of one-time codes for second-factor authentication, making them accessible across all your devices.

5. Private Notes for Password Entries: Allows you to attach private notes to password entries for added context or security.

6. Syncing Messages History: iCloud Keychain also syncs iMessage and SMS communication history, allowing access to message history across your devices.

7. Additional Synced Items on Macs: On Macs, iCloud Keychain automatically syncs settings for accounts listed in the Internet Accounts pane, signatures from Preview or Mail's Markup feature, and entries in the default macOS login keychain.

8. Accessibility Across Platforms: While primarily accessible within Safari on macOS, iCloud Keychain entries can be accessed from various places across Apple and third-party apps on macOS, iOS, and iPadOS devices, as well as through system settings. Additionally, on Windows, iCloud Passwords allows access to these entries, and there's compatibility with the Cloud extension for Edge or Google Chrome.

Overall, iCloud Keychain offers seamless syncing and accessibility of crucial data across Apple devices while ensuring security and ease of use for managing passwords and sensitive information.

Enable and Configure iCloud Keychain

Enabling and configuring iCloud Keychain across your Apple devices is straightforward, especially if you've already activated two-factor authentication for your Apple ID. Here are the steps to set up iCloud Keychain:

Mac (Ventura or later):

1. Go to System Settings: Click on the Apple logo in the top-left corner, then select "System Settings."

2. Access iCloud Settings: Click on your "Account Name," then select "iCloud."

3. Enable iCloud Keychain: Toggle on the "Password & Keychain" option.

Mac (Monterey or earlier):

1. Open System Preferences: Click on the Apple logo in the top-left corner and select "System Preferences."

2. Access Apple ID Settings: Click on "Apple ID."

3. Enable iCloud Keychain: Check the box next to "iCloud Keychain."

iOS/iPadOS (16 or later):

1. Access Settings: Open the "Settings" app.

2. Select iCloud Settings: Tap on your "Account Name."

3. Enable iCloud Keychain: Go to "Passwords & Keychain" and toggle on "Sync this iPhone/iPad."

iOS 15/iPadOS 15:

1. Open Settings: Launch the "Settings" app.

2. Access iCloud Settings: Tap on your "Account Name."

3. Enable iCloud Keychain: Go to "Keychain" and turn on "iCloud Keychain."

During this setup process, you might be prompted to enter your previously created iCloud Security Code or the passcode from another device already using iCloud Keychain. Once enabled, your iCloud Keychain will start syncing your passwords and sensitive data across your devices.

Now that you've set up iCloud Keychain, you can move forward to using it in Safari for managing passwords and other sensitive information.

Setting up iCloud Keychain without two-factor authentication requires a different approach and entails a more detailed process. Here's a guide to setting it up on your first device:

Setting Up iCloud Keychain on a Mac (Recommended as the First Device):

1. Open System Preferences: Click the Apple logo in the top-left corner, then select "System Preferences."

2. Access iCloud Settings: Click on "Apple ID," then select "iCloud."

3. Enable iCloud Keychain: Tick the checkbox for "Keychain" to enable it.

Setting Up iCloud Keychain on iOS/iPadOS (After Initial Mac Setup):

1. Open Settings: Launch the "Settings" app.

2. Access iCloud Settings: Tap your "Account Name."

3. Enable iCloud Keychain: Go to "Keychain" and turn on "iCloud Keychain."

Creating a Security Code (During Initial Setup):

1. You might be prompted to create a security code for iCloud Keychain during the setup process. Follow the on-screen instructions to create a security code.

Approving Additional Devices:

1. After the initial setup, additional devices can be approved to use iCloud Keychain through your first device.

2. On the additional device, sign in to iCloud using the same Apple ID.

3. A notification will prompt you to "Approve" iCloud Keychain on that device. Follow the instructions to proceed.

Setting up iCloud Keychain on a Mac as the first device ensures a smoother transfer of data to the iCloud keychain. Once the initial setup is done, follow the steps to approve additional devices. Once all your devices are set up, you can proceed to use iCloud Keychain in Safari to manage your passwords and sensitive information across all synced devices.

Enabling iCloud Keychain

Setting up iCloud Keychain on a Mac involves a few steps to ensure your keychain data syncs securely across devices. Here's a detailed guide:

Set up iCloud Keychain on Mac:

1. Adjust Security Settings (Optional but Recommended):

   - In Ventura or later: Go to System Preferences > Lock Screen.

   - In Monterey or earlier: Navigate to System Preferences > Security & Privacy > General.

   - Ensure that "Require password after screen saver begins or display is turned off" is set to a preferred time other than "Never."

2. Access iCloud Settings:

   - Go to System Preferences > Account Name > iCloud (Ventura or later).

   - For Monterey or earlier, access System Preferences > Apple ID > iCloud.

3. Enable iCloud Keychain:

   - Turn on "Passwords & Keychain" (Ventura or later) or select the "Keychain" checkbox (Monterey or earlier).

4. Enter Apple ID Password:

   - If prompted, enter your Apple ID password and click "OK."

5. Create iCloud Security Code:

   - As it's the first device for iCloud Keychain setup, you may be asked to create an iCloud Security Code.

   - Choose to enter a 6-digit numeric code or opt for greater security:

     - Use a Complex Security Code: Enter a password or phrase for higher security.

     - Get a Random Security Code: Let Apple generate a complex code for you.

     - Don't Create Security Code: Skip this step; you'll need to approve iCloud Keychain on other devices via another device.

   - Click "Next," re-enter the code if prompted, provide a mobile number for verification, and click "Done."

6. Keychain Sync:

   - macOS copies most login keychain items (Wi-Fi, app, internet, and web form passwords) to a new keychain called iCloud, which syncs across devices.

- Manage this keychain using Keychain Access (in /Applications/Utilities) or Safari's Preferences > Passwords.

- Note: iCloud Keychain and the login keychain are separate; changes in one won't affect the other.

Completing these steps ensures your keychain data is securely synchronized across devices, allowing you to manage passwords and sensitive information seamlessly.

When setting up additional devices for iCloud Keychain without two-factor authentication, you'll need to approve them using one of the following methods:

Approve Additional Devices:

1. Enable iCloud Keychain:

   - Access System Settings/System Preferences or Settings on the new device.

   - Turn on "Passwords & Keychain" (or "Keychain") as you did during the initial setup.

2. Choose Approval Method:

   - If using your iCloud Security Code:

     - Select the option labeled "Use Code" (in iOS/iPadOS).

     - Enter your iCloud Security Code when prompted.

     - You might need to verify via a verification number sent to your mobile phone via SMS.

   - If opting to approve from another device:

     - Choose the option "Request Approval" (in iOS/iPadOS).

- iCloud sends a request to all devices already using iCloud Keychain with the same Apple ID.

   - On those devices, a notification will appear; follow the prompts to approve the new device.

3. Sync iCloud Keychain:

   - Only after you've completed the approval process will your iCloud Keychain start syncing across all devices.

These steps ensure the secure syncing of iCloud Keychain across all your authorized devices, enabling seamless access to passwords and other sensitive information.

Use iCloud Keychain in Safari

Absolutely, using iCloud Keychain in Safari is a straightforward way to manage passwords and autofill data. Here's how you can enable and use these features on various platforms:

Enable iCloud Keychain Features in Safari:

On Mac:

1. Open Safari Preferences:

   - Go to Safari > Preferences.

2. Enable Autofill Options:

   - Select "AutoFill" and ensure the checkboxes for "User names and passwords" and "Credit cards" are checked.

3. Access Passwords:

- Click on "Passwords" at the top.

  - If prompted, enter your macOS user account password to unlock the passwords.

On iOS/iPadOS:

1. Enable Password Autofill:

   - Navigate to Settings > Passwords > Password Options.

   - Ensure "AutoFill Passwords" and "iCloud Passwords & Keychain" are turned on.

2. Activate Autofill in Safari:

   - Go to Settings > Safari > AutoFill.

   - Toggle on the switch for "Credit Cards."

Autofill Passwords:

On Mac:

- When you visit a website where you've stored login credentials in iCloud Keychain:

  - Click on the username or password field.

  - A pop-up menu will display with the available credentials. Click the appropriate one to autofill.

On iOS/iPadOS:

- When on a login page for a site with saved credentials:

  - Tap on the username or password field.

- The QuickType bar should display available credentials. Tap the relevant one to autofill.

Safari will then automatically fill in the username and password fields, streamlining the login process for websites where you've saved login details using iCloud Keychain.

Handling multiple sets of credentials in Safari across different platforms involves slight variations in the user interface:

Managing Multiple Credentials

On Mac:

- Deleting Autofilled Credentials:

  - If Safari autofills the wrong credentials, delete them from the username/password field.

- Choosing Specific Credentials:

  - Click in the username field to reveal a pop-up menu.

  - If multiple credentials are stored, click "Other Passwords for URL" to select the desired credentials.

On iOS/iPadOS:

- Selecting Credentials:

  - When multiple sets of credentials are available:

    - By default, a single option or two options may appear on the QuickType bar.

    - Tap the available options to autofill both the username and password fields.

- To access other stored credentials:

  - Tap the key icon or "Passwords" to reveal all available credentials for that site.

  - Authenticate using your passcode, Touch ID, or Face ID.

  - Locate and tap the desired credentials.

Troubleshooting Autofill Issues:

- If Autofill Doesn't Appear:

  - After deleting autofilled credentials:

  - On Mac: Click "Other Passwords" and manually choose the desired account or use the search function.

  - On iOS/iPadOS: Access the credentials by tapping the key icon or "Passwords," authenticate, then select the correct account manually.

Websites Blocking Password Saving:

- Some websites intentionally prevent password saving by browsers or password managers.

- Safari may attempt to bypass these restrictions automatically.

- Unfortunately, users don't have direct control over Safari's behavior in such cases.

By following these steps, you can manage multiple sets of credentials and troubleshoot any autofill issues you encounter while using Safari across Mac, iOS, and iPadOS devices.

Autofill Verification Codes

Autofilling verification codes adds an extra layer of security and convenience to the login process. Here's a breakdown of using verification codes with Safari across iOS, iPadOS, and macOS:

Setting Up Verification Codes:

- iOS/iPadOS and macOS support generating and autofilling verification codes for second-factor authentication.

- To set this up, you can refer to Glenn Fleishman's guide in the TidBITS article titled "Add Two-Factor Codes to Password Entries in iOS 15, iPadOS 15, and Safari 15."

Using Verification Codes in Safari:

- After entering your username and password on a website that requires a verification code, Safari can generate and autofill this code.

- Tap the field that requests the code; Safari will automatically create a code tied to the website's address.

- Simply fill in the generated code as you would with autofilled passwords.

Manually Accessing Verification Codes:

- If the code prompt doesn't appear in macOS or on the QuickType bar in iOS/iPadOS:

  - Use the iCloud Keychain entry to locate and copy the code manually.

  - Search for the relevant iCloud Keychain entry associated with the website's address.

  - Copy the code from the entry and paste it into the webpage form field where the code is required.

By utilizing Safari's capability to autofill verification codes or manually accessing them from iCloud Keychain entries, you can streamline the process of logging in securely across various platforms.

Storing new passwords or generating strong ones through iCloud Keychain is a convenient way to enhance security. Here's a detailed guide for storing and generating passwords on both Mac and iOS/iPadOS:

Storing New Passwords:

1. Store Existing Credentials:

   - If iCloud Keychain doesn't have your login credentials for a site:

   - Enter your username and password or use a third-party password manager.

   - Log in, and Safari will prompt you to save the password in iCloud Keychain.

   - Click or tap "Save Password" to store the credentials.

2. Store Additional Usernames/Passwords:

   - To store multiple username/password combinations for a site:

   - Delete autofilled credentials, enter new ones, log in, and click "Save Password" when prompted.

Generating Random Passwords:

1. Generate on Mac:

   - Ensure the Password field is empty.

   - Click in the field, and if a suggested password doesn't autofill:

- Click the key icon and select "Suggest New Password."

  - Safari generates a suggested password, showing only part of it as a "Strong Password."

  - Click "Use Strong Password" to accept it, or select an alternative from the pop-up menu.

2. Generate on iOS/iPadOS:

  - Ensure the Password field is empty.

  - If a suggested password isn't filled:

    - Tap the key icon or "Passwords," then select "Suggest New Password."

    - Safari displays a suggested password in a popover.

    - Tap "Use Suggested Password" to accept it or choose an alternative from "Other Options."

3. Fill Remaining Fields and Submit:

  - Fill in other required fields like Username.

  - Submit the form, and Safari saves your credentials automatically.

By following these steps, you can easily save new passwords or generate strong, unique ones using iCloud Keychain, enhancing security across your devices.

Storing and using credit card information via iCloud Keychain simplifies online purchases. Here's how to do it:

Storing Credit Card Information:

1. Saving Credit Card Details:

   - Enter your credit card number and expiration date into the respective form fields on a website.

   - When submitting the form, Safari will prompt to save the credit card details in your iCloud Keychain.

   - Confirm to save the information.

Using Stored Credit Card Information:

1. Filling Credit Card Details:

   - When prompted to enter credit card details during an online purchase:

   - Click or tap in the Credit Card Number field.

   - A pop-up menu or QuickType bar (on iOS/iPadOS) displays stored credit card options.

   - Choose the desired credit card from the menu/bar for autofill.

2. Selecting From Multiple Cards:

   - If you have multiple credit cards stored:

   - Safari presents a pop-up menu to select the preferred card, similar to handling multiple sets of credentials.

   - Choose the card you wish to use for the transaction.

This feature streamlines the process of entering and managing credit card information across various websites, making online shopping more convenient.

Using iCloud Keychain across different platforms and applications can be quite convenient. Here's how you can utilize iCloud Keychain on iOS/iPadOS and Windows:

iOS/iPadOS Apps:

- Accessing iCloud Keychain:

  - When using third-party apps on iOS/iPadOS:

    - Access the app's Sign-In screen.

    - Tap on the username or password field.

    - iOS/iPadOS might display relevant credentials in the QuickType bar.

    - Tap your credentials to autofill them.

  - If iOS/iPadOS doesn't display the right credentials:

    - Tap the key icon or the word "Passwords" to access the list.

    - Manually search and tap the correct credentials to fill them in.

iCloud Keychain on Windows:

- Using iCloud Passwords App:

  - On Windows, iCloud for Windows includes the iCloud Passwords app.

  - To use the app, set up Windows Hello on your Windows machine.

- Windows Hello requires a Trusted Platform Module or other security measures.

- Once set up, iCloud Passwords works like the Passwords view in Safari on macOS.

- It allows you to view and manage passwords synced from iCloud Keychain.

- You can copy usernames, passwords, and associated websites from this app.

These methods enable you to access and manage your iCloud Keychain entries on Windows and within various third-party apps on iOS and iPadOS, extending the convenience of password autofill and management across different platforms.

Absolutely, here's how you can view and manage your iCloud Keychain contents across different platforms:

On Safari for Mac:

- To Access Keychain Contents:

  - Open Safari and go to Safari > Preferences.

  - Click on "Passwords" (or navigate to System Preferences > Passwords in Monterey or later).

  - Authenticate with Touch ID or your user account password.

  - You can browse, search, view passwords, remove items, or add new ones.

On iOS/iPadOS Devices:

- To Access Keychain Contents:

- On iOS/iPadOS, go to Settings > Passwords.

- Enter your passcode, Touch ID, or Face ID.

- For credit cards, navigate to Settings > Safari > AutoFill > Saved Credit Cards.

- Swipe left on an entry to delete it.

Using Keychain Access on macOS:

- To Access Keychain Contents:

  - Open Keychain Access located in /Applications/Utilities.

  - Select iCloud from the list of keychains in the upper-left corner (if not visible, choose View > Show Keychains).

  - You can view, edit, and manage your passwords.

  - Keychain Access can also store secure notes but is only accessible on macOS.

While Keychain Access on macOS offers more detailed control, its interface might not be the most user-friendly. For most users, managing keychain contents through Safari's Passwords settings or via the iOS/iPadOS Settings app might be more intuitive.

Integrating iCloud Keychain with another password manager is possible, but they each serve distinct purposes and have their own sets of advantages. Here's how they differ and how they can complement each other:

Reasons iCloud Keychain and Third-Party Managers Coexist:

1. Platform Compatibility:

   - iCloud Keychain primarily serves Apple's ecosystem, while third-party managers often support cross-platform compatibility, including Windows, Android, and Linux.

2. Browser Support:

   - iCloud Keychain is limited to Safari on macOS, while third-party managers often support various browsers, providing autofill features across different platforms.

3. Expanded Features:

   - Third-party managers offer additional features like secure document storage, sharing specific passwords, software license storage, and broader cross-device syncing capabilities beyond Apple devices.

4. CVV Autofill for Credit Cards:

   - Unlike iCloud Keychain, some third-party managers offer the option to autofill CVV details for stored credit cards.

5. Password Sharing:

   - Sharing specific passwords securely with others is a feature available in various third-party managers, which is not supported by iCloud Keychain.

Using Both Simultaneously:

1. Confusion and Clutter:

- Storing credentials in both iCloud Keychain and another manager might lead to confusion during form filling and visual clutter.

2. Data Import and Sync Limitations:

- Due to limited access to Keychain data, transferring entries between iCloud Keychain and third-party managers is not straightforward.

- Password changes made in one manager won't automatically sync with the other, necessitating manual changes across platforms.

Considerations:

- Complementary Use:

- Users often opt to use a third-party manager as their primary password manager and leverage iCloud Keychain for specific functionalities or when working within Apple's ecosystem.

- Choosing Based on Needs:

- Your choice depends on your specific requirements: iCloud Keychain may suffice for basic usage within the Apple ecosystem, while third-party managers offer more expansive features and cross-platform support.

- Managing Expectations:

- Understanding the limitations and differences between the two allows for a more informed decision and smoother usage without overdependence on a single tool.

Ultimately, using both iCloud Keychain and a third-party password manager concurrently allows for flexibility and can cater to various security and convenience needs across different platforms and scenarios.

Use the iCloud Website

iCloud primarily ensures synchronization of data among your devices. Yet, beyond this, it hosts robust web applications accessible on the iCloud website. These encompass Mail, Contacts, Calendar, Photos, iCloud Drive, Notes, Reminders, Pages, Numbers, Keynote, and Find My. Additionally, for users who've enabled it, there's a unique News Publisher web app solely available on the iCloud website, absent from Mac or iOS/iPadOS versions.

While native Mac and iOS/iPadOS apps deliver enhanced power and convenience, there are compelling reasons to consider using the iCloud website:

1. Non-Apple Platforms: For individuals operating on Windows, Linux, Android, or other systems lacking native access to these apps, the iCloud site becomes indispensable. (Notably, iCloud Drive functions on Windows.)

2. Using Other Computers: Accessing your iCloud data becomes seamless when on someone else's or a public computer through the iCloud website.

3. Exclusive Settings: The website's Settings house certain unique features, notably the Data Recovery option, absent from native apps.

4. Find My for Lost Devices: When dealing with a lost or stolen iPhone or other devices, using Find My iPhone on the iCloud website, even from someone else's device or computer, becomes necessary to report, trigger sounds, or perform a remote erase.

Navigating the iCloud website involves signing in with your Apple ID, entering your password, and optionally selecting "Keep me signed in." After signing in, here are key actions to keep in mind:

1. Opening and Switching Apps: You have two options to access apps. You can either click on the app's icon from the home screen, which displays app names, or use the menu icon always visible on the screen. Clicking the menu icon allows you to choose the desired app from the popover that appears.

2. Settings and Signing Out: Your profile picture at the top provides a pop-up menu offering access to account settings and the option to sign out.

3. Finding Help: Clicking the menu icon and selecting "iCloud User Guide" opens a separate tab with helpful assistance. You can explore the table of contents or use the search icon for specific queries.

4. Customizing the Home Page: Personalize your display by clicking the menu icon and selecting "Customize Home Page." This allows you to edit, add, delete, or rearrange tiles representing apps. Click "Done" to finish customization.

The Mail Web App

The iCloud Mail web app mirrors many features found in Apple Mail for iOS/iPadOS, although it doesn't encompass the full functionality of macOS's Apple Mail. Surprisingly, iCloud Mail differentiates between Apple-managed items, labeled as "Mailboxes," and user-created ones, termed as "Folders."

Here's a breakdown of key actions and features within the iCloud Mail web app:

1. Managing Folders and Mailboxes: iCloud Mail segregates Apple-managed items as Mailboxes (e.g., Inbox, Sent, Trash) and user-created ones as Folders. Users can add, delete, rename, and rearrange these folders, including nesting them. Alphabetical sorting is the default for folders.

2. Layout and Preview: Upon selecting an item in the sidebar, its contents are displayed in the adjacent column. Further selection of an item within the mailbox or folder reveals its preview on the right. Users can adjust column widths by dragging the dividers.

3. Preferences and Customization: Various preferences in iCloud Mail are adjustable, such as managing aliases and setting rules. Access these preferences by clicking the gear icon in the sidebar, selecting Preferences, and choosing specific categories like General or Composing.

Additional functionalities within the iCloud Mail app:

- Viewing Messages: Clicking on a message displays its contents in the preview pane. Alternatively, double-clicking opens the message in a separate window.

- Message Actions: Icons at the top enable actions like composing, replying, flagging, deleting, and moving messages. Right-clicking a message or clicking the Reply icon reveals more options in a popover.

- Keyboard Shortcuts: iCloud Mail offers numerous keyboard shortcuts for efficient navigation.

- Aliases: Users can configure up to three aliases—extra icloud.com email addresses that direct messages to the main account—by accessing Preferences, then Accounts, and managing aliases.

- Rules: iCloud Mail supports server-based rules for incoming messages. Users can set up rules via the gear icon in the sidebar, granting some message-sorting abilities even on iOS/iPadOS devices, although less potent than Gmail's rules.

While iCloud Mail may not match the full feature set of desktop clients, it still offers robust functionalities for managing emails across different devices.

The Contacts Web App

In the Contacts web app, simplicity reigns, but there are two less-obvious features worth noting:

1. Gear Menu: Located at the bottom-left corner of the sidebar, the gear icon unfolds a menu offering Preferences, Import vCard, Export vCard, and other useful controls.

2. Add Contacts or Groups: Clicking the plus icon unveils a menu presenting options for creating a New Contact or New Group.

Moving to the Calendar web app, where you can efficiently manage events and appointments:

1. Sharing: To share or modify settings for a shared calendar, simply click the Share icon adjacent to the calendar. More details on this are covered in the Sync Your Calendars section.

2. Gear Menu: Situated at the lower-left corner, the gear icon provides essential controls like Preferences, New Event, and New Calendar.

3. Calendar List: Access the sidebar displaying a list of your calendars by clicking the Calendar List icon at the window's bottom. This allows for easy toggling of the sidebar's visibility.

4. Notifications: Check notifications, including events added by shared calendars or meeting replies, by clicking the Notifications icon at the window's bottom. The icon might display a number to indicate the quantity of notifications.

Both Contacts and Calendar web apps offer straightforward functionalities akin to their counterparts on Mac or iOS/iPadOS devices, providing ease in managing contacts and scheduling events across platforms.

The Photos Web App

In the Photos web app, you can engage with your iCloud Photos, although with more limited functionality compared to the Photos app on macOS or iOS/iPadOS. Key actions include:

1. Managing Media: Download, add to albums, or delete photos and videos. Select single or multiple items by holding ⌘ and clicking, then use icons like Download, Add, or Delete at the top.

2. Marking Favorites: Easily mark a photo as a favorite by hovering over its thumbnail and clicking the heart icon in the lower-left corner or using the heart icon at the top when the photo is open.

3. Uploading Photos: Specifically, JPEG format photos can be uploaded by clicking the Upload option at the top (videos can't be uploaded through the web app).

4. Working with Albums: Access albums through the sidebar or by clicking the sidebar icon. Create new albums, add photos to existing ones, or remove photos from an album using respective icons.

Transitioning to the Notes web app, akin to the Notes app in macOS and iOS/iPadOS:

1. Folder and Tag Management: Utilize the sidebar to select, create, or delete folders or tags. Notes can be dragged into folders displayed in the sidebar.

2. Creating Notes: Use the New Note icon to create new notes within the app.

3. Applying Styles: Apply various styles like Title, Heading, Subheading, Body, Monospaced, Lists, Bold, Italic, Underline, and Strikethrough via the Style icon.

4. Table Creation and Checklists: The app allows the creation of tables and turning selected paragraphs into checklists using respective icons.

5. Collaboration and Sharing: Collaborate with others by adding them to a note for simultaneous editing, facilitated by clicking the Share icon.

However, it's worth noting that while the Notes web app displays attachments, URLs, and text styles created elsewhere, it doesn't offer the ability to add these attributes. Additionally, note locking with a password, available in macOS and iOS/iPadOS, isn't supported in the web app, although it can unlock previously locked notes from other platforms.

The Reminders Web App

In the Reminders web app, the interface is user-friendly but lacks some functionalities present in the Mac or iOS/iPadOS versions. Notably, adding, removing, or sharing reminder lists can't be done through the web app; these actions require a Mac or iOS/iPadOS device.

The iWork Web Apps

Moving on to the iWork Web Apps—Pages, Numbers, and Keynote—these web-based versions are a marvel of engineering, incorporating a vast majority of features from their iOS/iPadOS and Mac counterparts directly within a web browser. Users familiar with iWork on other platforms will find these web app versions to be quite similar.

For detailed insights into any of these iWork apps, access the iCloud User Guide by clicking the menu icon, choosing iCloud User Guide, and navigating through the Table of Contents.

The iCloud Drive Web App

As for the iCloud Drive Web App, it offers file and folder viewing capabilities. Users can perform various actions using icons at the top, such as creating folders, uploading, downloading, deleting, and sharing items. Additionally, items can be rearranged through drag and drop functionality. Double-clicking Pages, Numbers, or Keynote documents opens them in the corresponding web app for seamless editing.

The Find My web app is a handy tool for locating your Apple devices like Macs, iPhones, iPads, AirPods, certain Beats models, and Apple Watches. It helps when your devices are misplaced or lost, and it can even assist in case of theft. You can use Find My to locate, play a sound on, lock, or erase the contents of the device. However, the Find My web app doesn't support the location of items like AirTags, which rely on device pairing and end-to-end encryption. For more details on locating hardware with an app, refer to the section 'Find Your Hardware with an App' later in the content.

The News Publisher Web App

The News Publisher web app caters to publishers, including individual bloggers, allowing them to contribute content to the News app on macOS, iOS, and iPadOS. This tool isn't readily visible to most iCloud users. To access and learn more about News Publisher, users need to sign up for the service, activating the News Publisher web app. Subsequently, they can submit news feeds for Apple's review and approval through the 'Publishing on Apple News' page.

Additionally, while not a traditional web app, the iCloud Settings page—accessible by clicking your profile picture in the upper-right corner and selecting iCloud Settings—provides access to various Apple ID settings. This includes managing language, time zone, storage, devices, Family Sharing, and other iCloud features. It also offers the option to restore certain items that may have been deleted from iCloud. More information about using the iCloud Website Settings Page is covered later in the content.

CHAPTER XII: FIND MY APP

Apple's Find My services encompass three primary categories, each designed for locating hardware and individuals in diverse ways, varying in permissions and consent levels. These are categorized similarly to how Apple organizes them within the native Find My apps for iOS, iPadOS, and macOS:

1. People: This feature enables users to share their location with friends, family, or others while also viewing the shared locations of those who have consented to sharing. It's about location sharing among individuals.

2. Devices: Under this section, all iCloud-linked computing and audio hardware is listed, including devices logged in by members of a Family Sharing group (if applicable). This includes iPhones, iPads, iPod touches, Macs, Watches, and supported audio hardware like AirPods, AirPods Pro, AirPods Max, and select Beats audio hardware. Tracking, sound playback, locking, displaying messages or rewards, erasing data, and monitoring battery levels are among the functionalities available for devices.

3. Items: This view incorporates AirTags and other items paired with an iPhone or iPad utilizing the Find My network. It covers third-party licensed devices from brands like Pebblebee, Chipolo, and Knog, including trackers and bike trackers, benefiting from the crowdsourced Find My network.

Across these categories (people, devices, and items), users can access the current location or inquire about it via Siri. Additionally, sound playback, locking, displaying messages or rewards, erasing data, and monitoring battery levels are available for devices and some items.

Notably, tracking for devices functions more reliably when they have an active cellular connection. iPhones, iPads with cellular modems, and Series 3 or later cellular Apple Watch models typically maintain a consistent network connection, ensuring better tracking capabilities compared to Wi-Fi, which might be intermittent and subject to login requirements or payment.

Activate Find My

To activate Find My Device or Find My Item, it's essential to ensure that Location Services is enabled on the device or item, and subsequently, Find My Device or the Find My network is turned on. Here's how you can enable Location Services on different platforms:

For macOS (Ventura or later):

1. Navigate to System Settings > Privacy & Security > Location Services.

2. Turn on Location Services if it's not already enabled (you may need to authenticate).

3. Scroll down to the bottom and click Details next to System Services.

4. Ensure that Find My Mac is also turned on.

5. Click Done.

For macOS (Monterey or earlier):

1. Go to System Preferences > Security & Privacy > Privacy > Location Services.

2. Click the lock icon to authenticate.

3. Select Enable Location Services.

4. Scroll down to System Services, click the Details button.

5. Ensure that Find My Mac is selected under "Allow System Services to determine your location."

For iOS/iPadOS:

1. Open Settings.

2. Go to Privacy & Security > Location Services.

3. Make sure Location Services is turned on at the top.

It's crucial to note that Find My Device and Find My Item track hardware in slightly different ways, and the process of enabling location updates may vary. Once Location Services is activated, you can proceed to turn on Find My Device or Find My Item based on your specific use case.

Turn on Find My Device

Sure, to ensure that Find My Device is active on your Apple devices:

For macOS:

- Ventura or later:

  1. Go to System Settings > Account Name > iCloud.

  2. Ensure that Find My Mac is turned on.

- Monterey or earlier:

  1. Navigate to System Preferences > Apple ID > iCloud.

2. Make sure Find My Mac is activated.

For iOS/iPadOS:

- iOS 16/iPadOS 16 or later:

  1. Tap Settings > Account Name.

  2. In earlier versions like iOS 15/iPadOS 15, tap Settings > Account Name > iCloud.

  3. Confirm that Find My Device is enabled. If not, toggle the switch to turn it on. You can also enable Send Last Location, which shares the device's location when the battery is low.

AirPods, Beats, and Apple Watches:

- These devices can be located through Find My Device if Find My iPhone is activated on the paired iPhone.

Checking Find My Network:

For macOS:

- Ventura or later:

  1. Go to System Settings > Account Name > iCloud.

  2. Click on Find My Mac and ensure that Find My Network is enabled.

- Monterey or earlier:

  1. Head to System Preferences > Apple ID > iCloud.

2. Click the Options button next to Find My Mac and verify that Find My Network is set to On.

For iOS/iPadOS:

- Go to Settings > Privacy & Security > Location Services > Share My Location > Find My Device.

- Make sure that Find My Network is activated. Also, turn on Send Last Location for added security.

Enabling Find My Network assists in locating devices even when they are offline or in a low-power state, enhancing the chances of recovering a lost device.

Understand Device and Item Locks

Enabling Find My Device initiates Activation Lock on devices equipped with screens. This security feature serves as a theft deterrent, preventing unauthorized erasure or setup of the device without the original iCloud account password that locked it. Even if a device is erased, starting from iOS 15/iPadOS 15, Find My can still be used to track it, enhancing security in case of theft or loss.

However, Activation Lock introduces an important consideration for buyers and sellers of used devices, detailed in the 'Check Activation Lock' section later in this book.

With your device configured, locating it becomes feasible using the Find My app on a Mac, iOS/iPadOS device, or via the iCloud website, all of which I'll describe in the following pages.

For Find My items, which lack screens or internet connectivity, Apple implemented the Pairing Lock. These items remain locked to the specific iPhone or iPad they are paired with, and unpairing requires physical proximity and access to unlock the associated iPhone or iPad.

Removing the Pairing Lock and disabling tracking without the associated iPhone or iPad is only achievable by removing the battery or disabling Find My on the item. However, without unpairing, the item may remain exclusively linked to the initial iPhone or iPad and cannot be used with another iPhone or iPad.

Deactivate Find My Device

To deactivate Find My Device, you can simply uncheck a box on a Mac or flip a switch on iOS/iPadOS, similar to how you activated it. Reasons for doing this include maintaining the device's location privacy, preparing to sell, gift, or recycle the device, or when signing out of iCloud entirely. Disabling Find My Device, especially before selling a device, is crucial to avoid activation lock issues, as discussed in the 'Check Activation Lock' section previously.

When you choose to turn off Find My Device, you'll be prompted to enter your Apple ID password and confirm the disabling of the Find My network. The device may request additional confirmation to ensure this action is intentional, as disabling this feature could potentially increase the risk if the device is lost or stolen.

As for deactivating Find My Items, like AirTags, which lack physical interfaces, or other Find My items with limited interaction, the process varies:

- For AirTags: Unscrew the battery cap and remove the battery following Apple's specific instructions. Refer to Apple's guidance for accurate steps.

- Third-party Find My items: Instructions for disabling or unpairing these items from devices can differ significantly. Refer to the respective manufacturers' websites for detailed instructions as they vary based on the device.

It's important to follow manufacturer-provided guidelines to ensure the proper deactivation of Find My network or unpairing of items from associated devices.

CHPATER XIII: FIND YOUR HARDWARE WITH AN APP

To locate your iCloud-enabled devices or items, like your iOS/iPadOS device, Mac, Apple Watch, or AirPod, the most convenient method is using the Find My app available for macOS, iOS, or iPadOS. This app is the sole means to track a Find My item or utilize the crowdsourced Find My network.

When using the Find My app, begin by opening it and, if prompted, authenticate your access. The app categorizes People, Devices, and Items into separate views accessible through tabs (macOS) or icons (iOS/iPadOS) in the upper-left or bottom corners, respectively. By clicking or tapping on Devices or Items, you can view your hardware's tracking status on a map.

Initially, both views display a map where iCloud attempts to locate all your devices or items. If you're part of a Family Group, the Devices view will also include all tracked devices of other group members, arranged by person below your own devices.

Each device or item listed displays its current location and distance beneath its name. Selecting a specific device or item allows you to isolate its location on the map.

The location might appear as a point with a shaded circle around it, indicating the estimated location and the potential margin of error. For certain devices or items, the initial location might be broadly defined, gradually narrowing down and zooming in as more location data is received.

On macOS, iOS, and iPadOS, selecting a device or item triggers a control panel to appear automatically, providing various options and functionalities. To access a similar control panel in the web-based Find My iPhone, click or tap the Info icon.

In the Find My app, several options are available to assist in locating or managing your devices or items:

- Play Sound: This feature plays a loud sound on the device, even if it's locked or set to silent. If the device is offline, the sound activates when it reconnects to the internet. You'll receive an email confirmation once the sound plays or the message is sent.

- Directions (devices): Offers navigation options, allowing you to get walking, driving, or transit directions to your device's location

- Find (AirTags): Exclusive to AirTags paired with an iPhone 11 or newer, this feature utilizes ultrawideband radios to pinpoint the AirTag's location within about 30 feet (10 meters), providing directional guidance using augmented reality. Adequate lighting is necessary for this function.

- Notifications:

  - Notify When Found: Alerts you by email when a device reconnects to the internet, especially useful if the device couldn't be located and was last seen more than an hour ago.

  - Notify When Left Behind: Helps prevent leaving devices behind by sending alerts based on specified locations, ensuring you don't forget your belongings.

- Mark As Lost: Locks the device, displays a custom message and contact number on the screen to assist in retrieval. Enabling this feature also suspends Apple Pay on the device. Upon recovery, Apple Pay can be reactivated with your Apple ID password, restoring synced cards.

- Remove This Device: Used when you no longer utilize a device. It's recommended to erase the device before removing it via Find My. Upon confirmation, Apple disables the device's Activation Lock once it's online.

These options in the Find My app provide various functionalities, from locating a device through sound to securing it with custom messages and remotely managing devices you no longer use.

Find Your Friends

The Find My Friends feature allows you to track the whereabouts of friends and family who've granted you permission to access their location data. This relies on their primary device, which can be an iPhone, iPad, iPod touch, or a cellular Apple Watch.

Here are steps to locate a friend who has granted you access using the Find My app on iOS/iPadOS. The process on macOS is very similar:

1. Open the Find My app on your iOS/iPadOS device.

2. Tap on 'People' to view the list of individuals whose location you're tracking.

3. Select a person's name from the list.

This action displays the individual's location on a map, accompanied by a panel featuring controls to contact them, obtain directions to their location, and set up notifications for specific events:

- Setting up Notifications:

  - To notify yourself:

- Change in Location or Absence at a Specified Place: Tap 'Add' > 'Notify Me.'

- To get alerts for arrival or departure: Tap 'When [Name] Arrives' or 'Leaves,' choose the relevant location, and set frequency if desired.

- For notifications when your friend is not at a specific location at a particular time: Tap 'Person Is Not At,' specify the timeframe and days, then create the notification. This can be handy for monitoring a child's presence at school or home.

- To notify your friend:

- Tap 'Add' > 'Notify [Friend's Name].' Select 'I Arrive' or 'I Leave,' set the location, recurrence, and tap 'Add.'

Granting Permission to Share Your Location:

- To permit a friend to track your location, return to the 'People' view in the Find My app, tap the plus icon, then 'Share My Location.' Enter their email address and send the request.

- To modify permissions for a friend, tap their name, and select 'Stop Sharing My Location' or 'Remove Name' to revoke access.

These steps allow you to access and manage location-sharing preferences, keeping track of your contacts or sharing your own location with trusted individuals.

Understand How iCloud Backup Works

iCloud Backup is a crucial feature for iOS/iPadOS users, ensuring the safety of vital data. It functions differently from computer backups due to app sandboxing and the lack of a browseable file system in iOS/iPadOS devices. Here's a breakdown:

1. Back Up Anywhere:

   - The convenience of backing up over Wi-Fi to Apple's servers lets you do it from anywhere, untethered from a computer.

2. Restore Sans Computer:

   - You can restore a device, even if data was corrupted or wiped during repairs, or set up a new device using existing data without needing a computer.

3. Differential Backups:

   - iCloud backups only duplicate new or changed data since the last backup, speeding up subsequent backups.

Considering these advantages, iCloud Backup is often recommended. However, it may consume significant storage space. You can manage this by expanding your storage, limiting backup content, or deleting older backups. Alternatively, using Finder or iTunes (for Windows) could be an option if you're low on space and unwilling to buy more.

What iCloud Backup Includes:

Here's a list of what iCloud Backup covers:

- Photos and videos taken on the device (if iCloud Photos isn't enabled)

- Device-specific photo albums (not those synced from a computer)

- App settings, documents, and Health data (on an iPhone)

- All account data, device settings, HomeKit configuration, Home screen setup, and folder organization

- Messages (iMessage, SMS, and MMS) if Messages in iCloud isn't enabled

- Call history, ringtones, and Visual Voicemail password

- Apple Watch backups

- Purchase history from Apple

Understanding what iCloud Backup encompasses allows users to safeguard crucial data and manage their backups efficiently.

Activate and Configure iCloud Backup

Configuring iCloud Backup for your iOS/iPadOS device is simple and crucial for safeguarding your data. Here's a step-by-step guide:

Enabling iCloud Backup:

1. Open Settings on your iOS/iPadOS device.

2. Tap your Account Name at the top.

3. Select iCloud > iCloud Backup.

4. Turn on "Back Up This iPhone" or "Back Up This iPad."

5. If prompted, tap OK to confirm.

Manual Backup (Optional):

After enabling iCloud Backup, you can manually start your initial backup:

1. Go to Settings > Account Name > iCloud > iCloud Backup.

2. Tap "Back Up Now" to manually initiate the backup process.

Monitoring Backups and Managing Data:

1. Access Settings > Account Name > iCloud.

2. You'll see an overview of your iCloud account's statistics at the top.

3. Tap "Manage Storage" to view details (similar to Figure 41, right).

4. Under "Backups," you'll see the total backup size for all your devices.

5. Tap "Backups" to view a breakdown by device.

6. Select a specific device to delete its entire backup or manage individual data types.

7. To disable future backups for a specific data type and delete its existing backups:

   - Tap the data type.

- Choose "Delete Documents & Data" (or "Delete Data").

  - Confirm the deletion by tapping "Delete."

After the initial backup, subsequent backups occur automatically daily, provided your device is connected to power, has an active Wi-Fi connection, and is locked. The last backup time is visible under Settings > Account Name > iCloud > iCloud Backup.

Managing iCloud Backup helps control storage usage and allows you to selectively remove specific data types from backups, ensuring efficient use of your iCloud storage.

Restore an iOS or iPadOS Device from a Backup

Restoring an iOS/iPadOS device from an iCloud backup involves several steps and patience due to the time it takes to complete. Here's a detailed guide:

Restoring from an iCloud Backup:

1. Verify Backup: Ensure you have a backup to restore from. Check via Settings > Account Name > iCloud > Manage Storage > Backups or in Finder/iTunes for Windows if connected to your computer.

2. Prepare for Erase:

  - Connect your device to a computer via USB.

  - Go to Settings > General > Transfer or Reset Device > Erase All Content and Settings.

  - Enter your passcode if prompted and confirm the erase by tapping "Erase Device" twice. You might also need your iCloud password if Find My Device was active.

3. Restore Process:

   - After erasing, turn on your device or set up a new device.

   - Follow the setup prompts for language, Wi-Fi, and other preferences.

   - Choose "Restore from iCloud Backup."

   - Enter your Apple ID and password.

   - Select the backup you want to restore from and tap "Restore."

4. Download and Restore:

   - The iCloud backup restoration process may take a while, as it downloads data. Be patient during this phase.

   - After the backup is downloaded, your device will restart and apply the backup.

5. Post-Restoration:

   - Upon unlocking, you might notice some apps are unavailable, and media libraries may be incomplete.

   - Apps and data will continue downloading in the background. Apps will show "Waiting..." and load with a circle-filling pattern as they download.

   - You can prioritize app downloads by tapping an app, pushing it up in the queue for faster download.

It's essential to keep your device connected to a stable Wi-Fi network and a power source throughout this process. Depending on your internet speed and the amount of data, the restoration duration can vary from several minutes to a few hours. Once all apps and data finish downloading, there won't be a notification, so periodically check the device for completeness.

CHAPTER IV: USE ICLOUD ON AN APPLE TV

Configuring iCloud features on your Apple TV is a straightforward process. Here's a step-by-step guide:

Set Up iCloud Account Features:

1. Access Settings: On your Apple TV, navigate to Settings.

2. Users and Accounts:

   - Scroll down and select Users and Accounts.

   - Choose your Account Name (Apple ID).

3. Sign In:

   - If your Apple ID isn't already listed, select Sign In.

   - Enter your Apple ID and password.

4. Configure iCloud Features:

   - Once signed in, you may be prompted to use the same Apple ID for iCloud Photos, Family Sharing, and associated AirPods from your iPhone. Choose accordingly and input your password if required.

5. Additional Options:

   - Under Users and Accounts > Account Name > iCloud, you'll find options related to iCloud:

   - One Home Screen: Enabling this ensures that your Home screen layout remains the same across all Apple TVs linked to your iCloud account.

- Photos: Toggle this on to access your iCloud Photos library on your Apple TV. You can customize settings further by enabling or disabling Show Memories and Shared Albums.

After completing this setup, you'll be able to access your photos via iCloud Photos on your Apple TV, and your Home screen layout will sync across all Apple TVs connected to your iCloud account. If you wish to view your photos, follow the steps outlined in the subsequent guide on using iCloud Photos on an Apple TV.

Here's a guide on utilizing various iCloud-related functionalities on your Apple TV:

View Shared Purchases:

- If you're part of Family Sharing, access movies and TV shows purchased by other family members on your Apple TV.

  - Navigate to Movies > Purchased > Family Sharing or TV Shows > Purchased > Family Sharing.

  - Select a family member to view their purchased content.

Use iTunes Match:

- If you've set up iTunes Match, access your Music library on your Apple TV.

  - Navigate to the Music app to listen to matched or uploaded tracks from your Music library, including playlists.

Use iCloud Photos:

- Set up iCloud Photos in the Settings app to access your photos and videos on your Apple TV.

  - Select Photos on the home screen to view your photos, videos, shared albums, and personal albums.

- You may be prompted to enable iCloud Photos upon first use. Additionally, view automatically generated Memories based on time, location, or faces.

Use AirPlay from iCloud:

- Utilize AirPlay from iCloud to stream media purchased from Apple or stored via iTunes Match directly from iCloud servers.

- Enable this feature by going to Settings > AirPlay and HomeKit on your Apple TV and ensure AirPlay is set to On.

- Once enabled, when your iOS/iPadOS device sends content to your Apple TV, it attempts to stream it from iCloud servers. If unavailable, it falls back to streaming from the device itself.

This method conserves your device's battery as it doesn't directly stream media and allows you to use someone else's Apple TV to play content from your iCloud account as long as your device is within range.

MANAGE YOUR ACCOUNT

Here's a detailed rundown of managing settings in the iCloud website:

Accessing iCloud Website Settings:

- Log in to the iCloud website and click your name at the top.

- Choose iCloud Settings from the menu to access various settings.

Settings Category:

Change Personal Information:

- Photo: Add or change the photo associated with your iCloud account.

  - Click Change Apple ID Photo.

  - To replace the image, click "Browse your device for a new image," locate the desired graphic, and click Upload.

  - Adjust the zoom level, reposition the photo, or change the rotation as needed.

  - Once satisfied, click Save.

Manage your Apple ID:

- Make changes to your Apple ID settings, password, or security settings.

  - Click the appleid.apple.com link under Apple ID Settings.

Sign Out of All Browsers:

- If you want to ensure all browser sessions, including the current one, are closed:

  - Click Sign Out of All Browsers.

Manage Apps That Can Look You Up:

- Control which apps allow others to find you by your email address for sharing documents.

  - Click Manage Apps under the Look Me Up by Email section.

These settings enable you to manage personal information, Apple ID settings, active sessions across browsers, and app permissions related to email lookups for sharing documents through iCloud.

Absolutely, here's a breakdown of the iCloud Storage and Data Recovery sections:

iCloud Storage:

- Click on Your iCloud Storage in the navigation bar to access a graph indicating various storage categories.

- The graph represents major storage categories, each color representing a different category. Detailed information is available on desktop and iOS/iPadOS devices.

Data Recovery:

- iCloud retains copies of specific data types (Contacts, Calendar events, Safari Bookmarks, and iCloud Drive files) for 30 days.

- Access Data Recovery from the navigation bar.

- Choose from Restore Files, Restore Contacts, Restore Calendars, or Restore Bookmarks.

File Recovery:

- For files, select the checkbox next to each file you wish to restore or use Select All to restore everything. Then, click Restore.

Other Data Recovery (Contacts, Calendars, Bookmarks):

- Individual restoration of contacts, events, or bookmarks isn't possible.

- Instead, you can restore the entire Contacts, Calendar, or Bookmark dataset to a previous archived state.

- Locate the item you wish to restore and click the Restore link adjacent to it.

- The selected data will be restored across all devices where that specific data type is enabled.

- iCloud archives your current data before restoration, allowing you to return to this state if needed later.

These features offer insight into your iCloud storage breakdown and provide a recovery option for specific types of data within a 30-day period.

Change Payment Settings

To change your payment settings for iCloud subscriptions or any other paid add-ons, here's how to do it on different devices:

On a Mac:

- For Ventura or later: Open the App Store app.

- Choose Store > Account.

- Click Account Settings at the top.

- Then, select Manage Payments.

For Monterey or earlier:

- Go to System Preferences.

- Click Apple ID.

- Navigate to Payment & Shipping.

On an iOS/iPadOS Device:

- Tap Settings.

- Tap your Account Name at the top.

- Choose Payment & Shipping.

These steps will allow you to update your billing address and credit card information for your iCloud subscriptions or any other associated paid services.

Check and Modify Your Storage Usage

Managing your iCloud storage across various devices is crucial. Here's how to check and modify your iCloud storage usage on both a Mac/PC and an iOS/iPadOS device:

On a Mac or PC:

1. In Ventura or later: Go to System Settings > Account Name > iCloud and click Manage at the top.

In Monterey or earlier: Navigate to System Preferences > Apple ID > iCloud and click Manage.

On Windows, open the iCloud app and click Storage.

2. In the dialog that appears, select a category on the left to see how much data it stores. For instance, Backups shows the total storage consumed by backups. To delete an item or all data from an app, select it and click Delete or Delete All Data. Confirm by clicking Delete.

On an iOS/iPadOS device:

1. Open Settings and tap your Account Name > iCloud.

2. If needed, tap Show All to reveal all apps using iCloud storage. Turn off the switch next to an app to stop it from using iCloud for storage.

3. To delete data stored in iCloud for an app, tap Manage Account Storage and select the app's name. Swipe left on an item to delete it individually, or tap options like Delete Documents & Data or Turn Off & Delete from iCloud to remove all data from that app.

These steps allow you to monitor your storage usage, delete unnecessary items, and manage your iCloud space efficiently.

Manage Account Recovery

The measures Apple offers for account recovery and digital legacy are quite thoughtful. Here's a brief explanation of each:

1. Apple ID Recovery Key: This recovery key provides an additional layer of security to regain access to your Apple ID account if you ever forget your password or lose access to your trusted devices. It's a standalone key, separate from your password, used during account recovery.

2. iCloud Data Recovery Service: This feature allows you to appoint trusted individuals who can assist you in regaining access to your iCloud data if you lose access to your Apple ID. These contacts can aid in recovering your iCloud information without having access to your Apple ID password directly.

3. Digital Legacy: This feature allows you to designate individuals who can access your iCloud data after you pass away. It's a way to ensure that chosen family members or trusted persons can retrieve your digital information from iCloud and manage your digital presence according to your preferences.

Both the iCloud Data Recovery Service and Digital Legacy contacts are methods to ensure that trusted individuals can assist in managing or retrieving your iCloud data under specific circumstances.

Decide on Using an Apple ID Recovery Key

Enabling the Apple ID Recovery Key provides a more streamlined and immediate method to reset your account password, offering convenience and bypassing the standard recovery process involving Apple's assistance. However, it's crucial to be mindful of the potential risk involved:

Advantages:

1. Instant Account Recovery: With the Recovery Key and associated two-factor authentication elements, you can reset your password immediately without involving Apple's support.

Disadvantages:

1. Risk of Unrecoverability: If you misplace or lose the Recovery Key and lack access to a trusted device or phone number, you may permanently lose access to your Apple ID account. There's no alternative recovery method beyond this key.

It's a trade-off between convenience and security. While the Recovery Key offers quicker access restoration, its irretrievability without the required elements poses a significant risk. Assessing your comfort with managing this level of responsibility is key in deciding whether to use the Apple ID Recovery Key.

Set Up Account Recovery Contacts

1. Eligibility Check:

   - Ensure your devices (iPhone, iPad, Mac, etc.) are updated to at least iOS 15, iPadOS 15, watchOS 8, or macOS 12 Monterey.

   - Verify that you're age-appropriate based on your country's requirements (typically 13 or older, but it might vary).

2. Two-Factor Authentication:

   - Confirm that two-factor authentication is enabled for your Apple ID. If not, set it up before proceeding.

3. Access Apple's Settings:

   - On your compatible device, navigate to the Settings app.

4. Recovery Contact Setup:

- Look for the section related to account recovery or iCloud settings.

5. Add Trusted Contacts:

  - Find the option to add or manage recovery contacts.

  - Follow the on-screen instructions to add individuals (friends, family members, etc.) as trusted recovery contacts.

  - You might need their Apple IDs or email addresses to send them invitations.

6. Invitation Acceptance:

  - Your chosen contacts will receive invitations. They need to accept these invitations to become your recovery contacts.

  - Once they accept, they'll receive specific instructions on how to securely store the recovery information.

7. Information Confidentiality:

  - Emphasize to your recovery contacts the importance of keeping this information secure and private.

Remember, the goal is to select individuals whom you trust explicitly, as they'll have access to critical information necessary to help you recover your iCloud account if the need arises.

iCLOUD SECURITY

In an era where digital landscapes hold our most precious information, safeguarding our digital sanctuaries is of utmost importance. Among the bastions of data security stands iCloud—a fortress protecting our valuable personal data. Understanding the core principles and practices underpinning iCloud security is pivotal in ensuring the sanctity of your digital haven.

The Cruciality of Account Security

The fundamental essence of iCloud security lies in fortifying the ramparts of your account against unauthorized access, data breaches, and potential threats. Think of it as fortifying the gates to a castle—any breach could lead to compromise, making it imperative to comprehend the potential risks lurking in the shadows when accounts fall into the wrong hands.

Delving into Data Protection Measures

The armor protecting your digital treasures within iCloud comprises a myriad of tools and methods. These include encryption—a shield rendering your data unintelligible to prying eyes—and secure data transmission, ensuring that your information traverses the digital realm unscathed. Apple's unwavering commitment to user privacy stands as a testament to their dedication in safeguarding your data, setting a benchmark for data protection across the tech landscape.

Understanding the intricate workings of iCloud's security mechanisms is akin to wielding a powerful arsenal, fortifying your digital bastion against potential threats. By comprehending the essence of account security and delving into the protective layers shielding your data, users can navigate the digital realm with confidence, knowing that their digital fortress stands strong against the tides of potential vulnerabilities.

Securing your iCloud account and protecting your privacy within it are critical steps. Here's a quick rundown of those essential security and privacy measures:

1. Strong Passwords:

  - Always use strong, unique passwords for your iCloud account. Avoid using easily guessable information like names or birthdays. Consider using a reliable password manager to generate and store complex passwords securely.

2. Two-Factor Authentication (2FA):

  - Enable two-factor authentication for an extra layer of security. This typically involves receiving a code on your trusted device or phone number when logging in from a new device or location.

3. Check Activation Lock:

  - Before purchasing a used Apple device, ensure it's not locked by Activation Lock. This ensures that the device is legitimate and not reported as stolen.

4. Privacy Settings:

  - Review and customize your privacy settings within iCloud. You can turn off syncing for sensitive data or restrict certain apps' access to your iCloud information.

5. Device Passcodes:

- Use passcodes or biometric locks (like Touch ID or Face ID) on your iOS/iPadOS devices. This adds an extra layer of security in case your device gets misplaced or stolen.

6. Regular Software Updates:

   - Keep your devices and apps updated with the latest security patches and software updates provided by Apple.

7. Backup and Recovery Options:

   - Regularly back up your iCloud data and consider setting up recovery options like recovery contacts or a Recovery Key for added security.

8. Avoid Phishing Attacks:

   - Be cautious of suspicious emails, messages, or links that could be phishing attempts trying to steal your Apple ID credentials.

9. Privacy Practices:

   - Practice good privacy habits, such as reviewing app permissions, limiting location sharing, and being mindful of what information you share online.

By combining these security measures with a proactive approach to privacy, you can better safeguard your iCloud account and the sensitive data stored within it.

Choose Mastering Strong Passwords

Choosing a strong password is indeed crucial for safeguarding your iCloud account. Here's a summary of the key points to keep in mind while creating a strong password:

1. Uniqueness: Ensure that your iCloud password is unique and not used for any other accounts or services. This prevents a breach in one service from compromising other accounts.

2. Strength: Aim for a robust password exceeding minimum requirements. Apple suggests at least eight characters with a mix of uppercase, lowercase, and digits. However, a longer password with a mix of characters (including symbols or punctuation) significantly enhances security.

3. Variation and Complexity: Consider using a passphrase or a randomly generated password with a combination of letters, numbers, symbols, and punctuation. Password managers can assist in creating and storing complex passwords securely.

4. Password Manager: Utilize a password manager like 1Password, Dashlane, or Bitwarden to generate, store, and manage strong, unique passwords for all your accounts. These tools also help in syncing passwords across devices and autofilling login details, enhancing convenience and security.

If you're ready to change your iCloud password, visit the Apple ID management page (appleid.apple.com), log in, and navigate to the settings to follow the instructions for changing your password. This proactive approach significantly bolsters the security of your iCloud account.

Two-Factor Authentication

Enabling two-factor authentication for your Apple ID significantly bolsters your account security. Here's a breakdown of what you can expect with two-factor authentication active:

1. Trusted Devices: Any device used to enable two-factor authentication becomes a "trusted device." These trusted devices are utilized, along with your password, to authorize new devices attempting to access your account. You can have multiple trusted devices linked to your account.

2. Signing In on Untrusted Devices: When logging in from a device that isn't yet deemed trusted:

   - You enter your username and password as usual.

   - An "Allow" prompt appears on all your trusted devices, displaying the location or origin from which the new device is trying to sign in. Once allowed on one trusted device, the prompt vanishes from the rest.

   - Simultaneously, a six-digit verification code appears automatically on the trusted device where you tapped "Allow." This code must be entered on the new device seeking access. Alternatively, if a trusted device isn't available, you can receive the verification code via SMS or an automated phone call.

3. App-Specific Passwords: Applications accessing your iCloud account's email, contacts, and calendars require app-specific passwords. This ensures secure access, just as with two-step verification.

By adding this extra layer of authentication, two-factor authentication mitigates potential threats from unauthorized access, phishing attacks, or compromised passwords, fortifying the security of your iCloud account.

Activation Lock

Activation Lock is a security feature available for iOS and iPadOS devices, Intel Macs equipped with T2 chips, Macs powered by M-series processors, and Apple Watches. This feature prevents unauthorized access by locking the ability to disable Find My Device, erase the device, or set it up under a different account without the correct iCloud credentials of the device owner.

Activation Lock doesn't have a distinct toggle to enable or disable; instead, it activates automatically when Find My Device is turned on for supported devices. If you plan to sell or give away a device with possible Activation Lock, ensure you deactivate Find My Device to disable Activation Lock beforehand.

For buyers of used Apple devices supporting Activation Lock, it's crucial to follow specific instructions provided by Apple for each device type to prevent purchasing a locked device unintentionally. Apple offers detailed guidelines for managing Activation Lock for various devices like Apple Watches, iOS and iPadOS devices, and Macs to avoid potential complications.

Security Key

Using a security key, though not a mainstream method, can greatly enhance security for those with specific security needs. It's a hardware dongle, typically USB-connected, that substitutes a numeric code with public-key cryptography to validate your identity. These keys are linked with a specific site during enrollment, providing robust security, but their usage comes with the risk of misplacement or loss.

For Apple ID accounts, instructions are available on selecting and employing a security key in Apple's guidelines titled "About Security Keys for Apple ID."

Additionally, when you activate two-factor authentication or two-step verification for your Apple ID, another security layer—app-specific passwords—comes into play. This feature applies solely to third-party apps accessing your iCloud account's email, contacts, and calendars (not other data types or Apple apps). You'll need to create unique passwords for each third-party app, enhancing security beyond your ordinary iCloud password.

Apple mandates undergoing two-factor authentication or two-step verification before generating app-specific passwords, ensuring dual-layer protection. Once generated for a specific app on a particular device, you won't receive prompts for a new password unless security settings change.

Essential Steps for Protecting Your Data

Protecting your iCloud data and maintaining privacy involves understanding encryption and taking practical steps to safeguard your information. Here's a rundown of some measures you can take:

1. Use Strong Passwords: Creating a robust and unique password for your iCloud account is the first line of defense. Avoid using the same password for multiple accounts to prevent widespread access if one password is compromised.

2. Enable Two-Factor Authentication: This adds an extra layer of security by requiring a secondary authentication method—like a trusted device or a verification code sent via SMS—to access your account. Even if someone knows your password, they can't log in without this secondary confirmation.

3. Passcode Protection for iOS/iPadOS Devices: Use a passcode on your iOS/iPadOS device to prevent unauthorized access. Additionally, configure the device to erase data after a certain number of unsuccessful passcodes attempts to protect sensitive information in case of theft or loss.

4. FileVault for Macs: FileVault encrypts the contents of your Mac's startup drive, making it unreadable without your account password. This protects your data even if someone has physical access to your device.

5. Understand Encryption and Data Storage: Be aware of which data is end-to-end encrypted, such as iMessage conversations and Health data, ensuring that it's locked to keys stored only on your devices.

Recognize that certain types of data like email, contacts, and calendars cannot be encrypted on the server using interoperable standards due to functionality requirements.

By implementing these steps, you can significantly enhance the security and privacy of your iCloud data, making it more resilient against unauthorized access or breaches.

Advanced Data Protection

Enabling Advanced Data Protection (ADP) for your iCloud account offers an additional layer of security by employing end-to-end encryption for various types of data. To activate ADP:

macOS Instructions:

1. Navigate to System Settings > [Your Account Name] > iCloud.

2. Locate and select Advanced Data Protection.

3. Click Turn On.

iOS/iPadOS Instructions:

1. Go to Settings > [Your Account Name] > iCloud.

2. Tap Advanced Data Protection.

3. Select Turn On Advanced Data Protection.

Account Recovery Setup:

Upon enabling ADP, Apple prompts you to ensure your account recovery methods are in place, as they won't be able to recover any data protected by ADP. Follow these steps:

1. Review and set up recovery methods if necessary, which might include using a recovery key or other verification methods.

2. If you have a recovery key, enter it, and proceed by entering your device's password or passcode when prompted.

3. Once successfully set up, you'll see the message "Advanced Data Protection is On."

Keep in mind that once ADP is active, Apple won't be able to retrieve any data you've protected with this feature. This added security is crucial, but it also means that safeguarding your recovery methods and keys becomes entirely your responsibility. After enabling ADP, Apple will send a confirmation email to your iCloud.com address.

This step significantly bolsters the security of your iCloud data by applying end-to-end encryption to a broader range of information stored in iCloud, enhancing protection against unauthorized access.

CHAPTER VIII: ICLOUD ALTERNATIVES AND COMPARISONS

1. iCloud by Apple:

- Integration with Apple Ecosystem: iCloud seamlessly integrates with Apple devices and services, offering smooth synchronization of data across devices.

- Privacy and Security: Apple prioritizes user privacy, employing end-to-end encryption for certain data and differential privacy techniques to protect user information.

- Limited Cross-Platform Support: While iCloud has a web interface, its functionalities are optimized for Apple devices, which might limit accessibility for non-Apple users.

2. Google Drive by Google:

- Cross-Platform Compatibility: Google Drive offers robust compatibility across various platforms, including Android, iOS, Windows, and macOS, providing broader accessibility.

- Collaboration Tools: Google Drive excels in collaborative features, allowing real-time editing, commenting, and sharing of documents among multiple users.

- Google Ecosystem Integration: Seamlessly integrates with other Google services like Gmail, Google Docs, and Google Photos, offering a cohesive user experience within the Google ecosystem.

3. Dropbox:

- Versatile File Syncing: Dropbox provides extensive file syncing capabilities across devices and platforms, allowing users to access files from anywhere.

- Third-Party App Integration: Offers integration with a wide range of third-party apps and services, providing flexibility and versatility in usage.

- Focused File Sharing: Dropbox specializes in file sharing and collaboration, offering robust sharing features for individuals and teams.

4. Microsoft OneDrive:

- Microsoft Integration: OneDrive integrates well with Microsoft Office Suite, offering seamless editing and sharing of Office documents.

- Cross-Platform Support: Available across various platforms, including Windows, macOS, iOS, and Android, providing versatility in usage.

- Collaboration and Productivity Tools: Offers collaborative features and additional functionalities tailored for business use, including SharePoint integration and enterprise-focused tools.

5. Amazon Drive by Amazon:

- Prime Membership Integration: Amazon Drive is linked to Amazon Prime, offering users additional storage and photo-sharing benefits.

- Limited Collaboration Features: Primarily focused on personal storage, lacking extensive collaboration tools compared to other services.

- Cost-Effective Options: Offers competitive pricing and plans, especially for Amazon Prime members, making it an economical choice for certain users.

Advantages of iCloud Over Competitors

1. Seamless Apple Ecosystem Integration:

   - Advantage: iCloud seamlessly integrates with Apple devices and services, ensuring a cohesive user experience for those within the Apple ecosystem. The synchronization of data across devices like iPhone, iPad, and Mac is seamless and built-in by default.

   - Impact: Users invested in the Apple ecosystem benefit from the convenience of having their data automatically synced across their devices without the need for additional setup or third-party applications.

2. Strong Emphasis on Privacy and Security:

   - Advantage: Apple prioritizes user privacy and security, employing robust encryption, differential privacy techniques, and a commitment to end-to-end encryption for certain sensitive data within iCloud.

   - Impact: Users concerned about data privacy often prefer iCloud for its strong stance on privacy and the company's transparency regarding user data handling practices.

3. Native Integration with Apple Apps and Services:

   - Advantage: iCloud's tight integration with native Apple apps like Photos, Contacts, Calendar, and Mail ensures a seamless user experience, with data automatically synced across these applications.

- Impact: Users find convenience in having their data automatically accessible and updated across various native apps without requiring separate setup or configuration.

Disadvantages of iCloud Compared to Competitors

1. Limited Cross-Platform Support:

  - Disadvantage: iCloud's functionalities are primarily optimized for Apple devices, leading to limited cross-platform support compared to services like Google Drive and Dropbox.

  - Impact: Non-Apple users or those using multiple platforms may find limitations in accessing and utilizing iCloud services on non-Apple devices or operating systems.

2. Less Collaborative Features and Third-Party Integration:

  - Disadvantage: iCloud offers fewer collaborative tools compared to competitors like Google Drive and Dropbox. Additionally, third-party app integration within iCloud is more restricted.

  - Impact: Users heavily reliant on collaborative work or requiring extensive third-party app integrations may find iCloud's collaborative features and ecosystem limitations less suitable for their needs.

3. Cost and Storage Plan Flexibility:

  - Disadvantage: iCloud's storage plans might be perceived as relatively less cost-effective or flexible compared to certain competitors like Google Drive, which offer more varied storage options.

  - Impact: Users seeking larger storage capacities at competitive prices might find more cost-effective alternatives outside the Apple ecosystem.

CHAPTER IX: FUTURE OF ICLOUD

1. Augmented Integration with Services:

   - Enhanced integration with Apple's services like Apple Music, Apple TV+, and Apple Fitness+, allowing for more seamless syncing of media content across devices and personalized recommendations based on usage patterns.

2. Advanced AI and Machine Learning Integration:

   - Leveraging AI and machine learning to improve data organization within iCloud, enabling better categorization, search capabilities, and automated tagging of photos, documents, and other content.

3. Expanded Collaboration Features:

   - Further advancements in collaborative tools within iCloud Drive, enabling real-time collaboration on a wider array of file types and enhancing productivity for teams and individuals working across different devices.

4. Enhanced Privacy Controls:

   - Providing users with more granular control over their data, allowing them to manage permissions and access settings for individual files, photos, or documents stored in iCloud, reinforcing Apple's commitment to privacy.

5. Extended Cross-Platform Support:

- Continuation of efforts to expand iCloud's functionality beyond Apple devices, potentially offering more comprehensive access to iCloud features on non-Apple platforms, enhancing accessibility for a broader user base.

6. Augmented Reality (AR) and IoT Integration:

- Integration of iCloud with AR applications and the Internet of Things (IoT), allowing for seamless data synchronization and interaction between AR experiences and connected IoT devices across the Apple ecosystem.

7. Improved Developer Tools and APIs:

- Further refinement and expansion of CloudKit and other developer tools, empowering app developers to leverage iCloud's capabilities more extensively, enhancing app experiences, and enabling seamless syncing across platforms.

8. Expanded Storage and Performance Enhancements:

- Potential increases in iCloud storage tiers and performance improvements, ensuring that users have ample space for their growing data needs and that syncing and access speeds remain optimal.

Printed in Great Britain
by Amazon